CAMPAIGN 379

THE EAST AFRICA CAMPAIGN 1914–18

Von Lettow-Vorbeck's Masterpiece

DAVID SMITH

ILLUSTRATED BY GRAHAM TURNER
Series editor Nikolai Bogdanovic

OSPREY PUBLISHING
Bloomsbury Publishing Plc

Kemp House, Chawley Park, Cumnor Hill, Oxford OX2 9PH, UK
29 Earlsfort Terrace, Dublin 2, Ireland
1385 Broadway, 5th Floor, New York, NY 10018, USA
Email: info@ospreypublishing.com
www.ospreypublishing.com

OSPREY is a trademark of Osprey Publishing Ltd

First published in Great Britain in 2022

A catalogue record for this book is available from the British Library.

Print ISBN: 978 1 4728 4891 8
ePub: 978 1 4728 4892 5
ePDF: 978 1 4728 4893 2
XML: 978 1 4728 4894 9

Maps by www.bounford.com
3D BEVs by Paul Kime
Index by Alan Rutter
Typeset by PDQ Digital Media Solutions, Bungay, UK
Printed and bound in Great Britain by CPI (Group) UK Ltd,
Croydon CR0 4YY

23 24 25 26 27   10 9 8 7 6 5 4 3 2

Artist's note

Readers may care to note that the original paintings from which the
colour plates in this book were prepared are available for private sale.
All reproduction copyright whatsoever is retained by the publishers.
All enquiries should be addressed to:

Graham Turner, PO Box 568, Aylesbury, Bucks, HP17 8ZX, UK

www.studio88.co.uk

The publishers regret that they can enter into no correspondence upon
this matter.

The Woodland Trust

Osprey Publishing supports the Woodland Trust, the UK's leading
woodland conservation charity.

www.ospreypublishing.com

To find out more about our authors and books visit our website. Here
you will find extracts, author interviews, details of forthcoming events
and the option to sign-up for our newsletter.

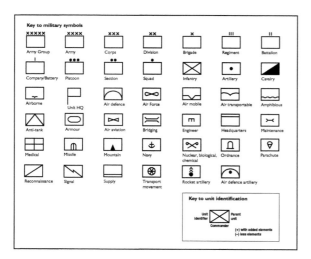

Front cover artwork: The 25th Royal Fusiliers at Mahiwa.
(Graham Turner)

Title page photograph: Damage to a railway carried out by
German troops in East Africa. (Public Domain)

CONTENTS

ORIGINS OF THE CAMPAIGN   5

CHRONOLOGY   8

OPPOSING COMMANDERS   10
British . German . South African

OPPOSING FORCES   13
Orders of battle

OPPOSING PLANS   19

THE EAST AFRICA CAMPAIGN   23
Part I: The British offensive . Part II: The railway war . Part III: The South African offensive
Part IV: The Germans withdraw . Part V: The final stage

AFTERMATH   91

THE BATTLEFIELDS TODAY   93

FURTHER READING   94

INDEX   95

European colonies in Africa, 1914

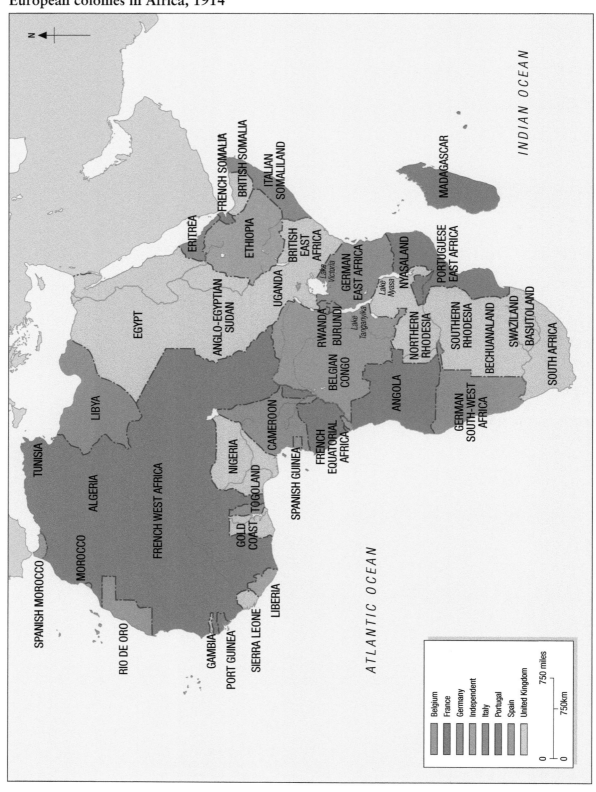

INDIAN OCEAN

MADAGASCAR

FRENCH SOMALIA

BRITISH SOMALIA

ITALIAN SOMALILAND

ERITREA

ETHIOPIA

BRITISH EAST AFRICA

PORTUGUESE EAST AFRICA

NYASALAND

UGANDA

GERMAN EAST AFRICA

Lake Victoria

Lake Nyasa

ANGLO-EGYPTIAN SUDAN

EGYPT

RWANDA

BURUNDI

Lake Tanganyika

NORTHERN RHODESIA

SOUTHERN RHODESIA

SWAZILAND

BASUTOLAND

BECHUANALAND

SOUTH AFRICA

BELGIAN CONGO

ANGOLA

GERMAN SOUTH-WEST AFRICA

LIBYA

TUNISIA

ALGERIA

MOROCCO

SPANISH MOROCCO

RIO DE ORO

FRENCH WEST AFRICA

NIGERIA

CAMEROON

TOGOLAND

GOLD COAST

SPANISH GUINEA

FRENCH EQUATORIAL AFRICA

GAMBIA

PORT GUINEA

SIERRA LEONE

LIBERIA

ATLANTIC OCEAN

Belgium
France
Germany
Independent
Italy
Portugal
Spain
United Kingdom

750 miles
750km
0
0

ORIGINS OF THE CAMPAIGN

The origins of Germany's East African colony are analogous to those of Britain's empire in India. Both were the product of private enterprises, and both were frowned upon by authorities back home. In both cases also, the motherland (or fatherland in Germany's case) came to be grateful for the unplanned additions to their empires.

While it was the East India Company that forced Britain to accept what it would later term its 'jewel in the crown', it was the work of a single man that was most responsible for the formation of German East Africa. Dr Carl Peters, in his capacity as head of the Society for German Colonization, secured a large number of treaties with African tribes, often relying on underhand tactics like getting chieftains drunk before asking them to sign a document. The result was that, from 1884, Germany steadily amassed a vast territory – far larger, in fact, than Germany itself.

Inevitably, this expanding empire caught the eye of the British, prompting the formation of British East Africa, with the specific aim of curbing German expansion on the continent. The 'scramble for Africa', where European nations fell over each other to claim huge tracts of the continent, was resolved in 1890 when a survey commission with British, French and German input settled on official borders.

Carl Peters was personally responsible for the acquisition of much of the territory that became German East Africa. A controversial figure, he was a believer in the concept of Social Darwinism, which stated that the strong would always profit at the expense of the weak. (ullstein bild via Getty Images)

134   PUNCH, OR THE LONDON CHARIVARI.   [September 22, 1888.

WOOING THE AFRICAN VENUS.
(Some way after Homer's Hymn to Aphrodite.)

[A Charter has just been granted to the Imperial British East Africa Company. This Company will now administer and develop a territory with an estimated area of about 50,000 square miles, including some of the most fertile and salubrious regions of Eastern Africa.]

The force, O Muse, and functions now unfold / Of Afric's Venus, graced with mines of gold ; / Who e'en in Bismarck lights love's furious fire, / And makes all men woo her with hot desire.   From all earth's nations, Frenchman, Por- / tuguese, / From Yankee shores and from all Europe's / seas, / Adventurous patriots crowd to seek and share / Love of the Libyan Venus. Three there are   Whose minds are mainly set upon that love : / The Briton, proud as Ægis-bearing Jove, / Who deems her indeviginate, her eyes / Being black and burning, like her own fierce / skies.

'Wooing the African Venus', which appeared in *Punch* on 22 September 1888, depicts various Europeans, headed by a British figure, attempting to seduce Africa. (Fotosearch/ Getty Images)

For a while, things settled down. Unlike Europe, which was a tinderbox of competing nations, the various colonies of Africa rubbed along peacefully. There was no appetite for armed conflict in pursuit of expansion, and far more effort was put into subduing the native populations, brutally in many instances.

Even when war loomed in Europe there was no desire to import it into Africa. Both terrain and climate were considered unsuitable for modern warfare, and there was a fear that if the ruling elites became preoccupied with fighting each other, the native populations might rise up in revolt. The business class had no interest in war either, seeing only disruption and ruin in their futures if blockades were imposed and armies stalked the land.

The Germans went to great lengths to try to avoid armed conflict in East Africa. This made sense from a commercial standpoint (and, of course, from a humanitarian one), but it was also a simple acceptance of reality. With potentially hostile colonies north, south and west, while to the east the Royal Navy ruled the waves of the Indian Ocean, there was little hope of German East Africa surviving a full-scale war intact.

The colony's governor, Heinrich Schnee, was personally committed to maintaining the peace. Aiming to keep his colony neutral, he declared its

The Herero Uprising, which started in 1904 in German South-West Africa, was ruthlessly quelled in what was later determined to have been a deliberate attempt at genocide. As many as 100,000 of the Herero perished. (The Print Collector via Getty Images)

ports, including Dar-es-Salaam and Tanga, to be 'open'. This meant they would refuse to accept or in any way help military vessels of any nation, in return for being considered non-combatants and, therefore, spared bombardment or blockade by the Royal Navy. The military garrison of Dar-es-Salaam was evacuated, and the capital moved inland.

In one of those tricky little events that can have almost endless ramifications, the German light cruiser SS *Königsberg* slipped out of Dar-es-Salaam before it was declared open. Subsequent action by this ship (it captured the British merchantman *City of Winchester* on 6 August) therefore made Dar-es-Salaam liable to retaliation and it was shelled by HMS *Pegasus* and HMS *Astraea* on 8–9 August 1914.

Despite this, Schnee remained fanatically opposed to war. Whether or not he would have been able to maintain the shaky peace in East Africa is an interesting debating point (the British were already eyeing up the Germans' most lucrative colony), but his efforts had been undermined by the arrival of a new military commander, Lieutenant-Colonel Paul von Lettow-Vorbeck. Though technically equals, von Lettow showed a complete disregard for the wishes of the governor and had no doubts about his duty once war broke out.

Dr Heinrich Albert Schnee (pictured left) with Paul von Lettow-Vorbeck, in Berlin, 1919. The two men, theoretically equal as civilian and military leaders of German East Africa, disagreed fundamentally on how the colony should respond to the outbreak of war in Europe. (Henry Guttmann/Hulton Archive/GettyImages)

The Germans were more bellicose in their approach to other, less-respected colonial neighbours, launching an operation on Lake Tanganyika to pry it from Belgian control and thus secure the colony's eastern boundary on 22 August, and attacking Maziua, in Portuguese East Africa, two days later.

In all likelihood, any form of neutrality was a dream. Britain hoped that some limited actions might provoke native uprisings in German East Africa, which might do the job of evicting the Germans with minimal effort, and a series of actions was authorized against the various German colonies. Troops were immediately called for from India, and although of variable quality, their numbers alone threatened to overwhelm von Lettow's limited resources.

How those resources were to be deployed became another bone of contention between von Lettow and Schnee. Schnee wanted them dispersed throughout the colony to counter the risk of civil unrest, while von Lettow wanted to concentrate near the border with British East Africa, ready to antagonize the British with a series of stinging, small-scale operations, including raids on the Uganda Railway. Towards the end of the war, von Lettow would encapsulate his strategy with a pithy statement: 'So long as we continued to resist, so long the enemy must pour resources into Africa and thus weaken his reinforcements in Europe. We were a knife in his side, and the more we turned it, the more he bled.'

Schnee's attempts at keeping the war at bay would prove futile, but it was not just the British who were to suffer. All of East Africa was about to start bleeding.

CHRONOLOGY

1914

5 August	News of declaration of war in Europe reaches East Africa.
6 August	The *Königsberg* captures the British merchantman *City of Winchester*.
8–9 August	HMS *Pegasus* and HMS *Astraea* bombard Dar-es-Salaam.
15 August	Germans capture Taveta.
20 August	British take control of Lake Nyasa.
22 August	Belgian ship *Alexandre Delcommune* sunk on Lake Tanganyika, giving Germans control of the lake.
24 August	Germans attack Maziua in Portuguese East Africa.
September	Germans raid around Uganda Railway.
1 September	First Indian troops (29th Punjabis, part of Indian Expeditionary Force C) arrive at Mombasa.
20 September	*Königsberg* sinks *Pegasus* in Zanzibar harbour.
16 October	Indian Expeditionary Force B sails from Bombay.
2–5 November	Assault on Tanga results in humiliating defeat for British forces.
4 November	*Königsberg* found in the Rufiji Delta.

1915

January	Von Lettow reorganizes *Schutztruppe* into three corps and recruits heavily.
18 January	German assault on fort at Jasin. Fort is taken, but at great cost.
March	German campaign of raids against Uganda Railway begins and lasts all year.
3 June	The monitors *Severn* and *Trent* arrive at the Rufiji having been towed 5,000 miles from the Mediterranean.
21 June	British launch raid on Bukoba, destroying radio mast.
28 June	German attack on Saisi.
6 July	*Königsberg* attacked by monitors.
11 July	*Königsberg* is scuttled after suffering serious damage in another attack by the monitors, but just days later her big guns are recovered by the Germans.

1916

6 February	Smuts replaces Smith-Dorrien as commander-in-chief of British forces.
9 February	Lake Tanganyika falls into Allied hands.
12 February	British attack on Salaita Hill a disaster.
8 March	British offensive, masterminded by Smuts, begins.

11 March	German positions on Latema and Reata hills assaulted.
15 March	Blockade runner *Marie* brings much-needed supplies to von Lettow.
12 April	Belgian offensive begins.
17 April	Van Deventer reaches Kondoa-Irangi.
10 May	German attack at Kondoa-Irangi starts ahead of schedule and confused night battle ensues.
21 May	Belgians take Rwanda.
27 May	Portuguese offensive on Rufiji stalls.
7 July	British capture Tanga.
15 August	British capture Bagamoyo.
25 August	British capture Morogoro.
4 September	Dar-es-Salaam captured.
19 September	Belgians take Tabora, the 'summer capital' of German East Africa.
October	Central Railway reopened by British after repairs.

1917

20 January	Hoskins takes command from Smuts.
May	British offensive from Kilwa and Lindi.
August	Von Lettow promoted to major-general.
22 September	Belgians capture Mahenge.
September–November	Zeppelin resupply effort (the 'China Show') fails.

15–18 October	German victory at Mahiwa/ Nyangao, the 'African Gettysburg'.
25 November	Germans cross into Portuguese East Africa. Portuguese defeated at Negomano.

1918

1–3 July	Battle of Namacurra.
26 September	Germans re-enter German East Africa.
1 November	Germans invade Northern Rhodesia.
25 November	Von Lettow surrenders.

Belgian troops march into Tabora on 19 September 1915. (Public Domain)

9

OPPOSING COMMANDERS

BRITISH

Michael 'Mickey' Tighe (1864–1925) had extensive experience of fighting in Africa, having first served in an expedition against the rebel chief Mbaruk in 1890. Further actions in Wa-Teita, Buddu and Ankole, as well as in Uganda and Unyoro, made him an obvious choice to take part in the East Africa campaign. An energetic and brave officer, Tighe was repeatedly decorated, winning the fabulously named Brilliant Star of Zanzibar medal. Educated at Sandhurst, his first unit was the Leinster Regiment, which he joined in 1883, and he saw action in the Burmese War and in the later Red Karen Expedition (also in Burma). By the start of the First World War his drinking was out of control and impacting upon his abilities, but his experience of the continent still saw him given overall command in East Africa for a brief period. He retired in 1921 with the rank of lieutenant-general, and died in 1925, at the age of just 61, after collapsing in a restaurant.

Sir Arthur Reginald Hoskins (1871–1942) was another product of Sandhurst, starting his military career with the North Staffordshire Regiment in 1891. He saw action in Egypt and was present at the fall of Khartoum, in

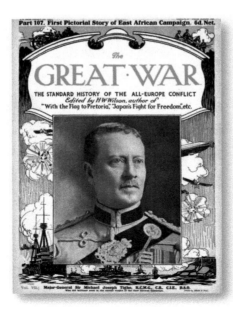

the Sudan, in 1898. He won the DSO in the Boer War, campaigned against the 'Mad Mullah' in Somaliland and, after a number of staff appointments, was named Inspector-General of the King's African Rifles in 1913. He fought on the Western Front in the opening years of the First World War, before being switched to East Africa.

GERMAN

Paul von Lettow-Vorbeck (1870–1964) was the son of a decorated Prussian officer, and was born just months before Germany became unified at the end of the Franco-Prussian War of 1870–71. Inculcated from his early years in the belief that independence of thought was a vital attribute in a commander, he would prove able to operate for years without direct orders from superiors. His military education began at the academy at Kassel, where he would meet one of his greatest friends, Tom Prince, who served under him in East Africa. Tall and strong, he was a gifted athlete despite being a chain-smoker. He fought in the Boxer Rebellion and the Herero Uprising, and he developed an appreciation for the tactics employed by the Boers against the British, at the same time as a contempt for British military leadership, both of which would colour his approach to command in East Africa. Prior to that, in German South-West Africa, he gained experience of bush fighting and also suffered an eye injury that may have resulted in his using a glass eye. Though right-wing in outlook, he was no Nazi and was mooted by Winston Churchill as a possible leader of post-Second World War Germany.

Seldom can a holiday have gone as badly as that planned by the oldest combatant in the East African theatre, **Kurt Wahle** (1855–1928). Coming to German East Africa to visit his son in 1914, the old general volunteered to come out of retirement when war broke out and he performed with honour almost to the end. Only a double hernia, after von Lettow had led his men back into German East Africa at the end of the war, saw him fall by the wayside. Though outranking von Lettow, he nevertheless served as one of his most able subordinates and was awarded the Iron Cross (First Class), as well as the *Pour le Mérite*.

FAR LEFT
Paul von Lettow-Vorbeck has been credited by some with inventing guerrilla warfare tactics. This is going too far, but he did show remarkable persistence and resourcefulness in holding out against a far superior enemy for the duration of the war. (Keystone/Hulton Archive/Getty Images)

LEFT
Though outranking von Lettow-Vorbeck, Kurt Wahle served as a loyal and highly effective subordinate until ill-health forced him to drop out during the last stage of the campaign. (Public Domain)

SOUTH AFRICAN

In contrast to the warlike upbringings of his fellow commanders in East Africa, **Jan Christian Smuts** (1870–1950) attended Cambridge University where he studied (and excelled in) law. After returning to his native South Africa, he pursued a career in politics until the Boer War dramatically changed the course of his life. Embracing the guerrilla tactics that proved so difficult for the British to counter, he became a formidable opponent and yet, after the Boer states had been absorbed into the British Empire, he would become a friend of Great Britain and was willing to serve for the empire in East Africa. Smuts had an instinctive awareness that swiftness of movement was essential in dealing with his weaker opponent, von Lettow, but was never able to put theory into practice. His appointment as South Africa's representative at an imperial conference in 1917 was an honour, but was at least partly motivated by his failure as a commander in East Africa. He favoured a less punitive peace with Germany following the war, but in that regard, his was a lonely voice.

A giant of a man, **Jacob 'Jaap' van Deventer** (1874–1922) served as a gunner in the Transvaal Artillery in 1896 and was a battery commander by the time the Boer War broke out. In that conflict he suffered a throat wound and spoke in a menacing whisper for the rest of his life. Having enjoyed a period of peaceful retirement on his farm, he was called back into service for the campaign in German East Africa. Van Deventer was aware of the danger of underestimating native troops and once in East Africa he cautioned his British counterparts, without success, not to despise their enemy. He ended the war as the commander-in-chief of British forces in East Africa, despite barely being able to speak English. 'He is cunning as an old fox,' commented a British officer, 'and does not make up his mind till the last moment. Then he acts like lightning; up to that moment he appears dense and slow. To him a decision is final; there is no swerving, no delay, no alteration of plan.'

OPPOSING FORCES

An extended war has seldom been fought between such mismatched opposing forces. Despite being outnumbered by three-, four- or even 10-to-one, the Germans kept an army in the field, undefeated, throughout the entirety of the war. Von Lettow only handed over his sword after being informed that the war in Europe was over – he surrendered, but was not defeated.

A large part of the reason for this was the nature of the theatre in which the war in East Africa played out, but it was also a factor of the armies involved. In difficult terrain, with often impossible weather conditions and a nightmare menu of tropical diseases and hostile wildlife to contend with, a small, hardened army was a positive advantage.

Von Lettow never had more than 15,000 men available at any one time, and usually had considerably fewer. The backbone of his army were the native troops, known as *askari*. The German commander was rare among officers in the theatre in holding no prejudices regarding skin colour, at least

The *Schutztruppe* had a long history of service. Depicted here is a range of uniforms as worn towards the end of the 19th century. (Bildagentur-online/Universal Images Group via Getty Images)

The German *askari* of 1914 were experienced, seasoned and brave. They were also comfortable in the extreme conditions of East Africa and able to retain fighting efficiency while the ranks of the British forces that pursued them withered under the onslaught of climate and disease. (Hulton Archive/Getty Images)

An infantryman of the 3rd King's African Rifles, in marching order, 1904. (Anne S. K. Brown Military Collection, Brown University Library)

as far as it impacted upon fighting ability. He valued the limited number of German NCOs and officers that he had at his disposal, but had a very high regard for the African men under his command as well.

The basic unit in von Lettow's *Schutztruppe* ('protection force') was the *Feldkompagnie*, or field company. Expanded from around 160 in peacetime to 200 after the outbreak of war (this was paper strength only), it was divided into three platoons of 60 men, with an additional, smaller, signals platoon. Each company had between 16 and 20 German NCOs and officers. There were 16 field companies as the war opened, totalling almost 2,000 *askari*, with 200 German officers and NCOs. These numbers were quickly expanded as the Germans awaited the opening blow of the campaign from the ponderous British. Railway and postal workers, volunteers and reservists were called up, and the number of companies swelled to nearly 40, including nine all-European *Schützenkompagnien* (*schütz* meaning 'sharpshooter', rather than *schutz* meaning 'protection' – a nod to the fact that these men were often members of shooting clubs). Additional units, including artillery, swelled numbers as well. Those numbers would peak at around 12,000 *askari* and 3,000 Germans. The Wamanyema were the main source of soldiers for the Germans, although by the end of the campaign, many

Wasukuma, initially enlisted as carriers, had traded their packs for a rifle and joined the ranks of the *Schutztruppe*.

Armament was a concern early in the war, with many of the *askari* having to make do with obsolescent rifles, which produced billows of black smoke, revealing a soldier's location to the enemy. Only six companies were armed with the superior 7.92mm Mauser Gewehr 98 at the start of the war, but better weapons were soon available after British routs and deliveries by blockade runners. Each company also had a pair of Maxim machine guns and most had two 37mm field guns as well. The machine gun would prove to be the dominant weapon on the battlefield, just as in Europe, despite the dramatic differences in the two theatres, but the Germans also benefited from the 10 big guns of the *Königsberg*, after the ship was scuttled in 1915.

The German army had up to 63 doctors, with support staff, assigned to it at any one time, but the real ace up its sleeve was the fact that its men were either native Africans, or had lived there for considerable periods of time and were thus less susceptible to tropical disease. It is not the case that they did not have any problems with sickness – von Lettow himself endured regular bouts of malaria – but compared to the British forces they were a picture of health. Where the African troops suffered most was in the highlands, where pneumonia would take its toll.

At the start of the war, the British had three battalions of the King's African Rifles (the 1st, 3rd and 4th), for a total of 21 companies and around 2,325 African troops, along with 73 British officers and NCOs. The men were armed with Lee-Metford or Lee-Enfield rifles, with one Vickers machine gun per company. This gave the British a remarkably similar number of native troops to the Germans, but unlike von Lettow, the British authorities were reluctant to expand the ranks of their native troops – Britain would find an army elsewhere in its empire, at least initially.

The first resource to be tapped was India. Von Lettow's stated goal was to tie down as many British troops as possible in East Africa, to prevent them from reaching the battlefields of Europe, but it is unlikely that many of the troops sent to Africa from India would ever have found their way to the Western Front. The men of Indian Expeditionary Force C numbered 4,000 and were earmarked to secure British East Africa, while the men of Expeditionary Force B (authorized before Force C but arriving later due to interminable logistical difficulties and a tedious and debilitating ocean crossing)

After Britain had found that British, Indian and even South African troops were not suitable for extended periods of service in East Africa, African troops, including the Gold Coast Regiment, were called upon. Here we see three decorated NCOs from the Gold Coast Regiment: Sergeant Granda Dikale, DCM, MM; Corporal Shumbo Lambe, DCM; and Corporal Etonga Etun, MM. (*The Gold Coast Regiment in the East African Campaign*, 1920)

numbered 8,000 and were tasked with nothing less than conquering German East Africa.

After these Indian troops had failed in battle and then shrivelled away under a relentless assault from tropical diseases (for some reason, the British had assumed their Indian troops would be immune to the dangers of the continent), Britain turned to South Africa. Under the command of the Boer War hero Jan Smuts, a South African army numbering some 30,000 was shipped to East Africa. Fresh from getting the better of the Germans with minimal fuss in German South-West Africa, Smuts had no doubt that he would make short work of them in the east as well. This army fared better than the Indians, but was similarly ravaged by disease and the South African public recoiled in horror at the sight of the men sent back home, in their thousands, to recuperate after mere months in the field.

The final phase of the war saw the British do what they should have done from the start, allowing Africans to do the fighting. As well as expanding the ranks of the KAR, they shipped over men from Nigeria and the Gold Coast. These experienced, highly effective fighting units were nonetheless tested by this new theatre of war.

Britain's allies in East Africa – Belgium and Portugal – fielded significant armies of their own, but of varying quality. The Belgian Congo was home to about 15,000 *askari*, many with little or no experience, but they performed well and earned the respect of their German counterparts for their ability to match the speed of the German units.

Portugal supplemented its 10 native companies with waves of expeditionary forces from Europe (totalling more than 19,000 men), which died in droves as soon as they reached Africa. The war was a miserable experience for all concerned, but especially so for the Portuguese expeditionary forces. They achieved next to nothing during the war.

ORDERS OF BATTLE

The situation changed constantly during the war, but the following are snapshots of some of the key moments.

INDIAN EXPEDITIONARY FORCES, 1914

INDIAN EXPEDITIONARY FORCE B

(Major-General A. E. Aitken)
Total strength: 7,972 troops, with 2,164 Indian
    Army followers
27th (Bangalore) Infantry Brigade
(Brigadier-General R. Wapshare)
2nd Battalion Loyal North Lancashire Regiment
63rd Palamcottah Light Infantry
98th Infantry
101st Grenadiers
Imperial Service Infantry Brigade
(Brigadier-General M. J. Tighe)
13th Rajputs
2nd Battalion Kashmir Rifles
Half of 3rd Battalion Kashmir Rifles
Half of 3rd Battalion Gwalior Infantry
Force Troops
61st King George's Own Pioneers
28th Mountain Battery RA (six guns)

Faridkot Sappers and Miners Company
No.25 and No.26 Railway companies

INDIAN EXPEDITIONARY FORCE C

(Brigadier-General J. M. Stewart)
Total strength: 3,000 troops, with 2,500 Indian Army followers
29th Punjabis
Four companies of Jhind Imperial Service Infantry
Four companies of Bharatpur Imperial Service Infantry
Four companies of Kapurthala Imperial Service Infantry
Four companies of Rampur Imperial Service Infantry
27th Mountain Battery (six guns)
Calcutta Volunteer Battery (six guns)
Volunteer Maxim Gun Company (four machine guns)

BATTLE OF TANGA, 3–4 NOVEMBER 1914

GERMAN FORCES

(Lieutenant-Colonel Paul von Lettow-Vorbeck)
Total strength: 935, 15 machine guns
1 *Feldkompagnie* (field company) (one platoon)
6 *Feldkompagnie*
13 *Feldkompagnie*

16 *Feldkompagnie*
17 *Feldkompagnie*
6 *Schützenkompagnie* (sharpshooter company)
7 *Schützenkompagnie*
8 *Schützenkompagnie*
Arriving late:
4 *Feldkompagnie*

BRITISH FORCES

(Major-General A. E. Aitken)
Total strength: approximately 5,500 engaged
101st Grenadiers
63rd Palamcottah Light Infantry
2nd Battalion Loyal North Lancs
3rd Battalion Kashmir Rifles (half battalion)
2nd Battalion Kashmir Rifles
98th Infantry
13th Rajputs
61st King George's Own Pioneers
Naval support:
HMS *Fox*
28th Mountain Battery (six guns, operating from the deck of *Bharata* or *Karmala*)

GERMAN FORCES IN EAST AFRICA, OCTOBER 1914

(Lieutenant-Colonel Paul von Lettow-Vorbeck)
Abteilung Wahle
(Major K. Wahle)
   Abteilung Rothe
   (Captain W. Rothe)
      Kompanie Tanga
      20 *Feldkompagnie*
      19 *Feldkompagnie*
   Abteilung von Liebermann
   (Captain E. von Liebermann)
      S *Kompanie*
      14 *Reserve-Kompanie* (Reserve Company)
      3 *Feldkompagnie*
      O *Kompanie*
      4 *Schützenkompagnie*
      9 *Feldkompagnie*
10.5cm howitzer, 10.5cm field gun, 4.7cm field gun
Abteilung von Ruckteschell
(Lieutenant W. von Ruckteschell)
      21 *Feldkompagnie*
      10 *Feldkompagnie*
Abteilung Göring
(Captain K. Göring)
      4 *Feldkompagnie*
      14 *Feldkompagnie*
      13 *Feldkompagnie*
      8 *Schützenkompagnie*
      17 *Feldkompagnie*
2 x 7.5cm mountain guns
Abteilung Köhl
(Lieutenant F. Köhl)
      6 *Schützenkompagnie*
      18 *Feldkompagnie*
Portuguese mountain gun
Etappenleitung (HQ)
(Captain P. Stemmermann)
      11 *Feldkompagnie*
Abteilung Kraut
(Major G. Kraut)
      25 *Feldkompagnie*
      2 *Feldkompagnie*
      3 *Schützenkompagnie*

      I *Kompanie*
   Abteilung Schultz
   (Captain Schultz)
      Etappenkompanie (Stage Company)
      5 *Schützenkompagnie*
10.5cm field gun
Westtruppen
(Captain T. Tafel)
Abteilung Schoenfeld
Lieutenant-Commander W. Schoenfeld (naval rank)
      2 *Schützenkompagnie*
      23 *Feldkompagnie*
      24 *Feldkompagnie*
Abteilung von Brandis
(Captain E. von Brandis)
      5 *Feldkompagnie*
Abteilung Aumann
(Captain H. Aumann)
      L *Kompanie*
      22 *Feldkompagnie*
Abteilung Poppe
(Captain M. Poppe)
      6 *Feldkompagnie*
Abteilung Otto
(Captain E. Otto)
      1 *Feldkompagnie*
      7 *Feldkompagnie*
      15 *Feldkompagnie*
      29 *Feldkompagnie*
C73 9cm field gun, 6cm field gun, 3.7cm field gun
Abteilung von Heyden
(Captain E. von Heyden-Linden)
      1 *Schützenkompagnie*
      Königsberg Kompanie

BRITISH MAIN FORCE IN EAST AFRICA, APRIL 1916

(General C. J. Smuts)
1st Division
(Major-General A. R. Hoskins)
1st East African Infantry Brigade
(Brigadier-General S. H. Sheppard)
      2nd Rhodesia Regiment
      20th Punjabis
      130th Baluchis
      Kashmir Battalion
2nd East African Infantry Brigade
(Brigadier-General J. A. Hannyngton)
      25th Royal Fusiliers (Legion of Frontiersmen)
      129th Baluchis
      40th Pathans
      3rd King's African Rifles
2nd Division
(Major-General J. L. van Deventer)
1st South African Mounted Brigade
(Brigadier-General M. Botha)
      1st South African Horse
      2nd South African Horse
      3rd South African Horse
      4th South African Horse
      9th South African Horse
3rd South African Infantry Brigade
(Brigadier-General C. A. L. Berrangé)
      9th South African Infantry
      10th South African Infantry
      11th South African Infantry
      12th South African Infantry
Divisional Troops

28th Mountain Battery
2nd South African Field Battery
4th South African Field Battery
11th Howitzer Battery
4th Armoured Car Battery
South African Motor Cyclist Corps
3rd Division
(Major-General C. Brits)
2nd South African Mounted Brigade
(Brigadier-General B. Enslin)
    5th South African Horse
    6th South African Horse
    7th South African Horse
    8th South African Horse
2nd South African Infantry Brigade
(Brigadier-General P. S. Beves)
    5th South African Infantry
    6th South African Infantry
    7th South African Infantry
    8th South African Infantry
Divisional Troops
    1st South African Field Battery
    3rd South African Field Battery
    No.8 (Calcutta) Battery
    No.13 Battery (2 x 5in. howitzers)
    No.5 Armoured Car Battery
    Volunteer Machine-Gun Company
    2nd Loyal North Lancs Machine Gun Company
    The Cape Corps
    5th Battery South African Field Ambulance
    1st Armoured Car Battery
    10th Armoured Car Battery
Army Troops
South African Scout Corps
Belfield's Scouts
Nos. 9, 10, 134, 38th Howitzer Brigade

BATTLE OF MAHIWA/NYANGAO, 15–18 NOVEMBER 1917

BRITISH FORCES

(Brigadier-General P. S. Beves)
No. 3 Column
(Brigadier-General O'Grady)
1st Bn, 2nd King's African Rifles
3rd Bn, 2nd King's African Rifles
Bharatpur Infantry
One section 27th Mountain Battery (two guns)
One section Stokes Mortar Battery (four mortars)
No. 4 Column
(Colonel H. C. Tytler)
25th Royal Fusiliers
30th Punjabis
3rd Bn, 4th King's African Rifles
259th Machine-Gun Company
Kashmir Mountain Battery (four guns)
One section Stokes Mortar Battery (four mortars)
Force Reserve
8th South African Infantry
3rd Nigerians
One company 61st Pioneers
One section East African Pioneers
One section No. 3 South African SA Battery (two 13-pounder guns)
One subsection RMA Heavy Battery (one 4in. gun)
134th Howitzer Battery (one 5.4in. howitzer, two 5in. howitzers)
Nigerian Brigade
(Lieutenant-Colonel Mann)
1st Regiment

2nd Regiment
3rd Regiment
4th Regiment
Gambia Company
Nigerian Battery (four 2.95in. guns)

GERMAN FORCES

(Lieutenant-Colonel Paul von Lettow-Vorbeck)
3, 4, 9, 10, 11, 13, 14, 17, 18, 19, 20 and 21 *Feldkompagnien*
4, 6 and 8 *Schützenkompagnien*
14 *Reserve-Kompanie*
Tanga Company
O and S *Kompanien*
One *Königsberg* gun
One 4.1in. field howitzer
Two 75mm mountain guns
One 70mm gun
One 47mm gun

BRITISH FORCES IN EAST AFRICA, MARCH 1918

(Major-General J. L. van Deventer)
Norforce
(Brigadier-General E. Northey)
Colonel G. Hawthorn's Column
    2/1st King's African Rifles
    3/1st King's African Rifles
Colonel C. Clayton's Column
    2nd Cape Corps
Independent Battalions
    2/4th King's African Rifles
    3/4th King's African Rifles
Forces Reserve
    1/1 King's African Rifles
    2/4 King's African Rifles
    4/1 King's African Rifles
    Northern Rhodesia Police
Pamforce
(Brigadier-General W. F. S. Edwards)
Colonel R. Rose's Column
    Gold Coast Regiment
    4/4th King's African Rifles
    King's African Rifles Mounted Infantry
Colonel G. Giffard's Column
    1/2nd King's African Rifles
    2/2nd King's African Rifles
Force Troops
    Gold Coast Regiment Mounted Infantry
    58th Vaughan's Rifles
Mobforce
    3/2nd King's African Rifles
General Reserve (Lindi)
Colonel T. Fitzgerald's Column
    1/3rd King's African Rifles
    2/3rd King's African Rifles
    3/3rd King's African Rifles
Garrison Troops
Dar-es-Salaam
    2nd West India Regiment
    Arab Rifles
    British West Indies Regiment
Coastal Ports
    1/7th King's African Rifles
Tabora
    2/6th King's African Rifles
British East Africa
    1/5th King's African Rifles
    1/6th King's African Rifles

OPPOSING PLANS

The aims of the multiple protagonists in East Africa were varied. There was the usual thirst for new territories, a desire not to 'miss out' on what was likely to be a redrawing of borders after the war, grandiose dreams of empire-building and pragmatic acceptance of limited possibilities.

Of all the combatants, it was the Germans who had the most intriguing and complex approach to the war. The primary driving force behind their presence in Africa had changed over the years. From a brutal regime highlighted by liberal use of the savage *kiboko* whip, the Germans had transformed into a more paternalistic presence. With the arrival of Schnee as governor, in 1912, emphasis switched to educating the natives and the German colonies became more progressive, within the limitations of the era.

At the same time, Germany was still intent on expanding its empire. The territories owned by Great Britain were considered off-limits, but the Portuguese to the south and Belgians to the west were fair game. These territories would be combined into a great German Central Africa, a new Fatherland.

The major problem with this was that Britain was unwilling to accept the status quo in Africa. Germany would have liked nothing more than a form of détente with Britain on the African continent, allowing them to focus their meagre resources on the Belgian Congo and Portuguese East Africa, but Britain's determination to export the European war made this impossible.

German East Africa was also riven by a philosophical disagreement that was never fully resolved throughout the war. Governor Schnee wanted to remain neutral and was willing to accept almost any indignity from the British as long as it prevented the horrors of war from being visited upon his colony. The military commander, von Lettow-Vorbeck, had very different ideas. Although well aware that he did not have the forces necessary to actually defeat the British, he saw it as his duty as a German officer to tie up as many British troops as possible, thus preventing them from deployment on the battlefields of Europe.

Von Lettow's tactics therefore served a subtle and unusual strategy, one that his opponents had great

Although Germany's long-term ambitions stretched to raising the imperial flag over a vast transcontinental colony (German Central Africa), von Lettow's aims during the war were more modest – to simply occupy as many resources of the British Empire as possible. (Amoret Tanner/Alamy)

German *askari* drilling prior to the outbreak of war. Responsibilities mostly included suppression of the native population, but they proved to be elusive and tenacious opponents on the battlefield. (Photo by Haeckel collection/ullstein bild via Getty Images)

difficulty in comprehending. He would antagonize the British, demanding a response from them, but always remaining out of their grasp. He would stand and fight when it suited him, and even mount limited offensives when the risk was low, but his overriding concern was not protecting territory, nor was it defeating his opponent. It was merely to keep his army intact. This required a herculean effort, especially as he was cut off from resupply from Europe for the bulk of the war. What supplies and equipment did fall into his hands had to be husbanded very carefully.

British plans were simpler, but vastly more difficult to realize. German territories in Africa were not greatly appealing to the British. Cameroon, Togo and German South-West Africa were not seen as having much potential, but German East Africa was a different story. Considered agriculturally promising, the British very much liked the idea of adding it to their possessions on the continent.

The main problem faced by the British was their unwillingness to arm the native population. The drawing in of troops from elsewhere in their vast empire was the obvious solution and it gave Britain a greatly superior force, numerically at least, to that employed by the Germans. The size of the British Army in East Africa, however, would become one of its weaknesses – cumbersome, slow and unimaginative, it would lumber after the fleet-footed Germans for the next four years.

Farmhands working on a sisal-agave plantation. The agricultural potential of German East Africa was particularly tempting to the British, who saw the war as an opportunity to expand their African empire. (Photo by Haeckel collection/ullstein bild via Getty Images)

The British war effort would go through multiple phases. Initially, echoing the optimism of the early days of the war in Europe, a short, sharp offensive was envisaged. Using imported troops from India, the British planned a large-scale invasion at Tanga, and then intended using the port as a base to move inland along the Northern Railway, before cutting southwards and then back to Dar-es-Salaam, the German capital.

When this initial strategy failed, a huge infusion of troops effectively handed the war over to the South Africans. Under the command of Jan Smuts, von Lettow's army itself became the target. Smuts aimed to pin the German commander, encircle him, and annihilate him in a decisive battle. With his overwhelming superiority of numbers, Smuts had reason for optimism, but his strategy demanded two elements that would prove elusive: he needed an opponent who could not move faster than him and one who was obliging enough to stand and fight. The employment of thousands of mounted troops promised to make the former a reality (until the tsetse fly laid waste to Smuts' mounted columns), but von Lettow was never going to allow himself to be cornered.

The King's African Rifles were a match for the German *askari*, but the British initially proved unwilling to employ their East African troops. Events during the early stages of the war would force a rethink and the KAR became the mainstay of the army. (Culture Club/ Getty Images)

In the final stage of the war, Britain called in troops from West Africa as well as expanding the ranks of the KAR, handing over the war once more, this time to native Africans, with help from the Belgians and, to a lesser extent, the Portuguese. The final strategy was little more than a pursuit of von Lettow's dwindling 'army' until it was hounded out of German East Africa, allowing the British to temporarily claim victory… before the Germans returned and even had the nerve to invade British Northern Rhodesia.

The Belgians and Portuguese had similar aims. Their goals were merely to be involved, so that they might protect their own territories and possibly scoop up scraps as they fell from the negotiating table after the war. The Belgians made a genuine contribution, despite being viewed with great suspicion by the British, while the Portuguese performed so badly they became known as the 'Pork and Beans' to the British and the *shenzi ulaia* ('trashy soldiers') to the German *askari*.

Gold Coast infantry in Togo, August 1914. Having gained experience on the other side of the continent, they were an obvious choice for bringing eastwards when the initial British strategy of employing largely Indian and South African troops had failed. (Public Domain)

German East Africa, north of the Rufiji, 1914

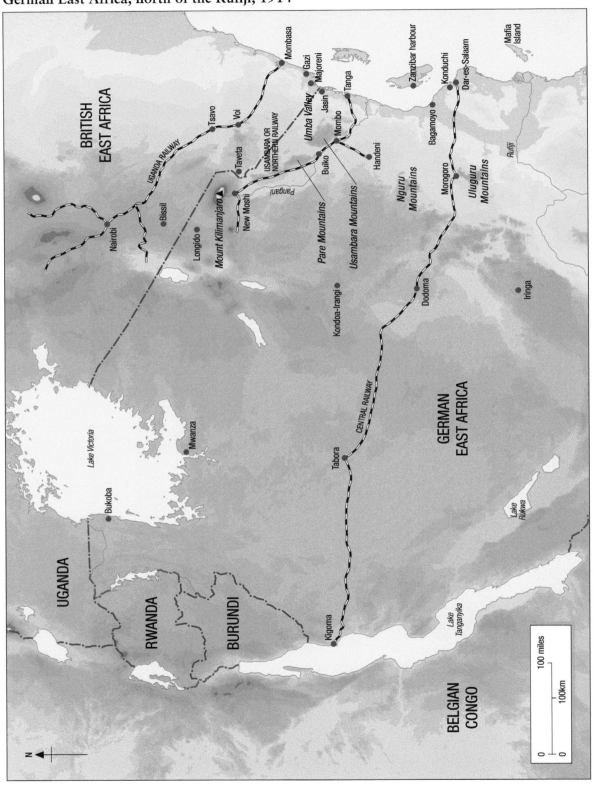

THE EAST AFRICA CAMPAIGN

PART I: THE BRITISH OFFENSIVE

Indian Expeditionary Force B was just one of six such corps sent out from the subcontinent over the course of the war. Expeditionary Force A was sent to the Western Front, B and C were directed to East Africa, D joined the Mesopotamia Campaign, E headed for Sinai and Palestine, and F saw action at the Suez Canal. Force C, commanded by Brigadier-General James 'Jimmie' Stewart and tasked with securing British East Africa, started arriving on 1 September, when the 29th Punjabis reached Mombasa. Force B, with the daunting job of taking control of the huge territory of German East Africa, did not even leave Bombay (after sweltering in troop ships for weeks) until 16 October. Commanded by Major-General Arthur Aitken, IEF B was comprised of two brigades: the 27th (Bangalore) Brigade and the Imperial Service Infantry Brigade.

Before Britain's reinforcements arrived, the initiative in East Africa lay with the Germans, and they did not waste their opportunity. Governor Schnee wanted to disperse troops about the interior of his vast colony, to guard against civil unrest, but von Lettow, convinced the British would mount an invasion, wanted to be prepared to defend the coast and also launch provocative raids into British East Africa. The more the sleeping lion could be goaded, he reasoned, the greater its response would be, and he had spelled this out when he declared, '... it is our military objective to detain the enemy... if it could by any means be accomplished. This however was impossible if we remained neutral.'

Consequently, he stationed seven of his companies at Konduchi, a day's march from Dar-es-Salaam, and on 15 August launched an attack on the British post of Taveta. This strategically useful position would be the obvious launchpad for a future British thrust into German East Africa, and it was taken at the cost of a single man. Tom Prince, a close friend of von Lettow's, commenced fortifying the position with the intention of holding it.

Events followed a similarly low-key pattern elsewhere. To the south, the British took control of Lake Nyasa by firing a single shot into the *Hermann von Wissmann*. The slightly surreal nature of the war, which was to be a feature throughout, was emphasized by the fact that the commander of the German vessel, Captain Berndt, was a friend of the commander of the British ship, Captain Rhoades, and reacted with indignation to the attack.

Things went better for the Germans on another lake, although on a similarly small scale. The sinking of the Belgian ship *Alexandre*

The light cruiser *Königsberg* became the focus of a huge naval effort, although its successes in the early days of the war had been extremely limited. (Library of Congress)

Delcommune, on 22 August, gave the Germans control of Lake Tanganyika. A raid on a post in Portuguese East Africa two days later meant Germany had attacked two neutral neighbours. Von Lettow was indeed stirring up a hornets' nest.

The German commander had already planned ahead with remarkable prescience. Anticipating a war in which he would be unable to rely on regular resupply from Europe, he had scouted the territory he would be working in. German East Africa was around twice the size of Germany, and his task was immense, but by getting a firm picture of the territory in his mind, he would be able to plan ahead when the time came for the British to take the initiative. More than this, he was able to prepare ammunition dumps and organize the growing of crops to keep his army fed and supplied.

At sea, the *Königsberg* was becoming a *bête noire* for the British back home, none more so than Winston Churchill, in his capacity as First Lord of the Admiralty. Having made a nuisance of itself by taking the *City of Winchester* on 6 August, it made itself public enemy number one, at least as far as the Indian Ocean was concerned, by sinking the *Pegasus* while it was undergoing repairs in Zanzibar harbour. The *Königsberg* was a lion on the prowl, and Churchill put together a hunting party to bag it.

The 'Destroy *Königsberg* Squadron' achieved for the Germans at sea almost exactly what von Lettow hoped to do on land – tying up a disproportionately large amount of the enemy's resources. After the German ship took refuge in the Rufiji Delta, where it awaited coaling, the British deployed ship after ship to hunt her down, starting with HMS *Chatham* and her sister ships HMS *Dartmouth* and HMS *Weymouth*. The *Königsberg* would never sail on open water again, but it would be months before she was finally destroyed.

Although von Lettow's eventual success would give him an air of invincibility, the early months of the war were actually a mixed experience for the Germans. A move against Mombasa, with 600 men, held early promise. The garrison of the British fort at Majoreni was forced to withdraw on 25 September, but a ragtag group of freed prisoners and hastily recruited men, along with a small number of KAR soldiers, allowed the British to hold the Germans at Gazi, about 25 miles south of Mombasa, and the offensive stalled. One last assault, on 8 October, was launched just after the British had received a reinforcement of three KAR companies, which tipped the balance decisively.

To the south, Major Erich von Langenn-Steinkeller moved on Karonga, in Nyasaland. His 800-strong force, including 5 *Feldkompagnie* (FK), was granted a golden opportunity when the British commander, Captain Barton, took the bulk of his 400 rifles on a scouting mission, leaving just 70 to guard Karonga. Fortunately, the defenders held up the German attackers long enough for Barton to send troops to the rescue. The British commander, anticipating a German retreat, then laid a trap and caught them unawares as they withdrew, and 5 FK suffered 70 per cent casualties on the day.

Things petered out as von Lettow was forced to concede that these early moves had been too costly and had achieved little. He now put his efforts into preparing for the upcoming British offensive; against the wishes of Schnee, he concentrated his men in the north east. Taveta was garrisoned

Among the ships sent to destroy the *Königsberg* was HMS *Chatham*, whose 6in. guns outpunched the German vessel's 4.1in. armament. (The original French caption at top right is intended to refer to HMAS *Sydney*, a Chatham-class light cruiser which forced aground SMS *Emden* in the Cocos Islands in November 1914.) (Arkivi/Getty Images)

H.M.S. Croiseur léger CHATHAM
qui aida à couler l'"Emden"

S.Cribb. Southsea

591

A·N
PARIS

with two all-European *Schützenkompagnien*, four *Feldkompagnien* protected Rombo, and three more were based at New Moshi. Four field companies took up positions at Longido, with three tasked to protect Tanga. Two more companies roamed the Northern or Usambara Railway. It added up to 3,500 experienced men, but would von Lettow be able to concentrate his scattered units when the British made their move? There was doubt over whether the blow would fall on Tanga or Dar-es-Salaam, and there were not enough men to mount a strong defence of both at the same time. Everything would depend on how quickly the British moved.

The Battle of Tanga

Von Lettow could draw comfort from his knowledge of the British performance in the Boer War. The British soldiers had been brave, but the generals had been ponderous, and the idea of a lightning descent on the coastline of German East Africa was almost comical.

The leader of Indian Expeditionary Force B, General Aitken, had never commanded in battle, and the men under his command had been hastily and haphazardly cobbled together in the face of competing demands from other theatres. With Force B initially comprising the 16th Poona Brigade, Aitken was temporarily in the strange situation of commanding a force that did not exist when that brigade was repurposed for the Middle East. To say units were scratched together to rebuild his command would not

The port of Tanga. Fearing mines in the harbour, the British commanders chose not to land troops here and instead opted for far less convenient options. (Keystone-France/Gamma-Rapho via Getty Images)

The streets of Tanga in pre-war German East Africa, scene of fierce fighting during the British invasion. In the background, the Bismarck Memorial can be seen. (Haeckel collection/ullstein bild via Getty Images)

be an exaggeration but, despite this, his mission orders were ambitious: 'The object of the expedition under your command is to bring the whole of German East Africa under British authority… you should first occupy Tanga… When this move has had its moral effect on the Germans occupying the hinterland of Tanga, Force C should if possible threaten Moshi from the Tsavo side.'

It is worth noting that the initial plans for Force B had been far more modest. Occupying Dar-es-Salaam and destroying the port's radio mast was all Aitken's command had originally been asked to accomplish. Interrupting German communications and depriving them of a naval base for operations in the Indian Ocean had somehow morphed into a desire to conquer an area considerably bigger than Germany itself.

Whether influenced by the casual nature of these orders, or perhaps impressed by his temporary elevation to major-general, Aitken was over-confident from the start. His low opinion of African soldiers would be problematic, and he also seemed strangely unaware of the inferior quality of the bulk of his own troops. With IEF B was the colourful Captain Richard Meinertzhagen, a Baron Munchausen-esque dreamer and fantasist who may have concocted many of the escapades he later wrote about. His opinion of IEF B, however, was biting: 'They constitute the worst in India. I tremble to think what may happen if we met serious opposition.'

Von Lettow was planning to offer serious opposition, but there was still uncertainty over where the British would land. On 22 October, Captain

Baumstark relayed a report that Tanga was to be the target, but von Lettow was wary of committing his men too soon. He bided his time.

There was little reason to hurry. The transport ships carrying IEF B were limited to the speed of the slowest vessel in the convoy, and that condemned them to a two-week crossing of the Indian Ocean at the snail's pace of just seven knots. To make matters worse, many of the men had been embarked two weeks prior to setting off, and illness ran rife in the crowded, sweltering conditions below decks. Still, on 30 October the fleet reached Mombasa, and the officers discussed their options. The seemingly obvious move of putting the troops ashore to recover from their ordeal was discounted, and this strange decision also denied them an opportunity to drill together. Instead, they were moved directly to their objective. The first land touched by the feet of IEF B in weeks would be the beaches of hostile territory.

Complicating matters further, Captain Caulfeild of HMS *Fox*, who would be the senior naval officer for the operation, was insistent that Tanga be treated as an open port. This would require notice being given of an intention to land troops. This might not cause much of a problem if the notice period was not too long, but with von Lettow's reinforcements able to travel to Tanga by train, there was not a lot of time to waste. The narrow-gauge railway offered its own problems, however. A locomotive could only haul seven carriages, and that was enough for just one company, although if equipment was left behind more men could be squeezed in. Bringing reinforcements from New Moshi, 150 miles away, would take time.

Another view of the harbour at Tanga, showing the jetty. Unloading of equipment would have been considerably quicker if the British had used these facilities during their landings. (Haeckel collection/ullstein bild via Getty Images)

A spanner was thrown in the works when HMS *Goliath*, which was to have supported the landing alongside *Fox*, suffered engine failure and had to drop out. Undeterred, Aitken decided to make his move.

There were around 900 buildings in the port of Tanga. The harbour itself was too shallow for large vessels, so lighters would be used to ferry the troops to shore. The landing order was set as the 13th Rajputs, the 61st KGO Pioneers, the 2nd Battalion Kashmir Rifles, the 3rd Battalion Kashmir Rifles (half-battalion) and the 3rd Battalion Gwalior Infantry (half-battalion).

Only one platoon of 17 FK was in Tanga when the invasion fleet was spotted at 06:30hrs on 2 November. The district commissioner, Dr Auracher, met with Captain Caulfeild on the *Fox* an hour later. Caulfeild gave the Germans two and a half hours to surrender. Auracher sent telegrams to both Schnee and von Lettow, and then joined the platoon of 17 FK in his dual capacity of lieutenant in the *Schutztruppe*. Meanwhile, the deadline to surrender passed and there was no sign of activity from the British fleet. At 10:45hrs, Caulfeild informed Aitken that no surrender had been forthcoming and then, after their men had been suffering at sea for weeks, the British commanders started to consider which beach to land on.

The lack of planning in the operation would be amusing were it not for its tragic consequences. Fear over the possibility of the main harbour being mined led to a small, muddy beach, labelled 'Beach A', being chosen. Troops were transferred to lighters at 18:00hrs and they started to move towards the shore at 22:00hrs. Given the advanced hour, the 13th Rajputs and 61st KGO Pioneers were the only troops landed that night. They were ordered to secure the town, with the rest of IEF B scheduled to follow the next day.

The lighters encountered a reef some distance off the beach and had to unload their cargoes early, forcing the already tired men to wade to shore through deep water. The laborious process eventually saw Brigadier-General Michael 'Mickey' Tighe ready to move inland with the 13th Rajputs and four of the six companies of the 61st Pioneers. By now, it was quarter past five on the morning of 3 November.

Von Lettow had waited until troops started to land before ordering wholescale reinforcements to Tanga. It was a gamble, but the landing may have been a feint, or a joint operation might have been planned for Dar-es-Salaam. Still, the remainder of 17 FK had already undertaken the four-mile march from its base at Kange, and more units were ordered to march to Tanga, while 6 FK, 6 *Schützenkompagnie* (SchK) and parts of 1 FK were packed onto a train from Moshi.

The *askari* of 17 FK had taken up a strong defensive position along a railway cutting, and they opened fire on Tighe's men as they moved tentatively inland. Tighe brought up reserves and extended his line, aiming to outflank the German position, but the troops of the 61st Pioneers were not combat troops and were shaky at best. It would not take much to tip the balance against Tighe's men, but for a while at least they held their own against the well-positioned German forces, and within an hour 17 FK was on the verge of pulling back as its ammunition ran dangerously low.

At 07:30hrs, everything changed with the arrival of the first German reinforcements, under Lieutenant Merensky. The new troops (having travelled by train from New Moshi) allowed the Germans to extend their line, outflanking the 61st Pioneers, who broke. Tighe was also forced to withdraw the 13th Rajputs, who had become pinned by the machine guns of the defending troops. Haphazard fire support from *Fox* did more damage to the German hospital than any of their troops, and as the *askari* pressed their advantage, the 13th Rajputs were routed. Tighe's men found themselves back on their landing beach, badly shaken.

The disorganized nature of the British assault now cost them dearly. After sweeping for mines, the landing beach for subsequent units was switched to Beach B and by 11:30hrs the men of the Imperial Service Brigade had landed. Showing a shocking lack of urgency, Aitken did not plan to attack again until the following morning, 4 November, after the remainder of his troops had been landed. Even worse, there was no reconnaissance made of the situation in Tanga, which had changed dramatically. The Germans, feeling unable to withstand a concerted effort from the troops massing on the beaches, had pulled out of the town. Tanga was undefended, except for a few light patrols, and the British could have simply marched in and taken possession.

It was to be a fleeting opportunity. More German units were arriving at Kange all the time, with von Lettow reaching Tanga in the early hours of 4 November. The German commander instantly showed the British how

A close personal friend of von Lettow-Vorbeck, Tom Prince was born in 1866 and was a plantation owner as well as an officer in the *Schutztruppe*. He died at the Battle of Tanga. (Bildagentur-online/ Universal Images Group via Getty Images)

it was done by jumping on a bicycle and riding into town to get first-hand knowledge of the situation. Having found the British were still limiting activities to their landing sites, von Lettow ordered his men to reoccupy the town and prepared his defences.

These initially built upon the dispositions of the first day's fighting, with 6 FK setting up a defensive line to the east of the town, but the extra units at his disposal allowed him to plan for a counterattack, and he placed 16 and 17 FK, along with a composite company made up of police and several other small groups, echeloned to the right, under the command of Captain Baumstark. These troops would be able to deliver a 'right hook' counterattack if, as von Lettow anticipated, the British came on in their traditional frontal assault. To the rear, he kept his best troops, the 7th and 8th *Schützenkompagnien* and 13 FK, under Prince. The arrival of 4 and 9 FK, as well as a pair of ancient guns, was also anticipated.

While the British laboriously prepared for their assault, the Germans enjoyed freshly cooked sausages and drank the milk of the coconuts that grew abundantly in the area. Von Lettow began to doubt if the British were going to rouse themselves for an attack that day, and pondered his chances of success if they did. He was well aware that in directly ignoring orders from Governor Schnee, he would face a court-martial if he was defeated. Not only that, the entire defence of German East Africa would unravel if the army under him, numbering only slightly fewer than 1,000, was destroyed.

Against the risk, he weighed the opportunity: 'I knew the clumsiness with which English troops were moved and led in battle,' he commented in his memoirs, 'and it was certain that in the very close and completely unknown country in which the enemy would find himself directly he landed, these difficulties would grow to infinity.'

At 15:00hrs, word finally came that the British were advancing. As von Lettow had hoped, they came in a traditional battle line, ponderous and clumsy. The German commander could not have known that the British 'advance' had been underway for nearly three hours by the time it became apparent to the defenders of Tanga. Part of the reason for the painfully slow progress was the fact that Aitken had his men drawn out in an old-fashioned battle line. The difficult country (coconut trees, rubber trees, sisal, thick undergrowth and bush grass higher than a man's head) made it almost impossible to maintain the line as the troops moved forward unsteadily. The men deployed included the 101st Grenadiers, the 63rd Palamcottahs, the 2nd Battalion Loyal North Lancashire Regiment and one and a half battalions of Kashmir Rifles. Following behind were the badly shaken 13th Rajputs and the 98th Infantry, with the 61st Pioneers in the rear.

When the battle commenced, the results were mixed. The 63rd Palamcottahs wilted under machine-gun fire and many of them fled for the rear, the confusion added to by the appearance of swarms of angry bees, disturbed from their hives (the battle is sometimes referred to as 'the Battle of the Bees').

The flight of the 63rd Palamcottahs appears to have unnerved the 98th Regiment, who became unwilling to move forward. There is controversy over whether they were actually ordered to plug the gap left by the Palamcottahs (Aitken attempted to cover up his lamentable performance in his official report), but it is clear that they did not do so.

Elsewhere, steadier troops, plus sheer weight of numbers, were having an effect. The Loyal North Lancs and Kashmir Rifles, along with some of

BATTLE OF TANGA, SECOND DAY, 4 NOVEMBER 1914

Shown here is the fighting from the second day of the Battle of Tanga.

GERMAN
A. 6 *Feldkompagnie* (field company, FK)
B. 16 FK
C. 17 FK
D. Composite Company
E. 7 *Schützenkompagnie* (sharpshooter company, SchK)
F. 8 SchK
G. 13 FK
H. 4 FK

TOTEN ISLAND

CUSTOMS HOUSE

TANGA BAY

MISSION STATION

EUROPEAN TOWN

TA

NATIVE T

E

7

F

9 G

VON LETTOW

10

H

Note: the base map occupies an area of approximately 4,000 yards by 3,000 yards.

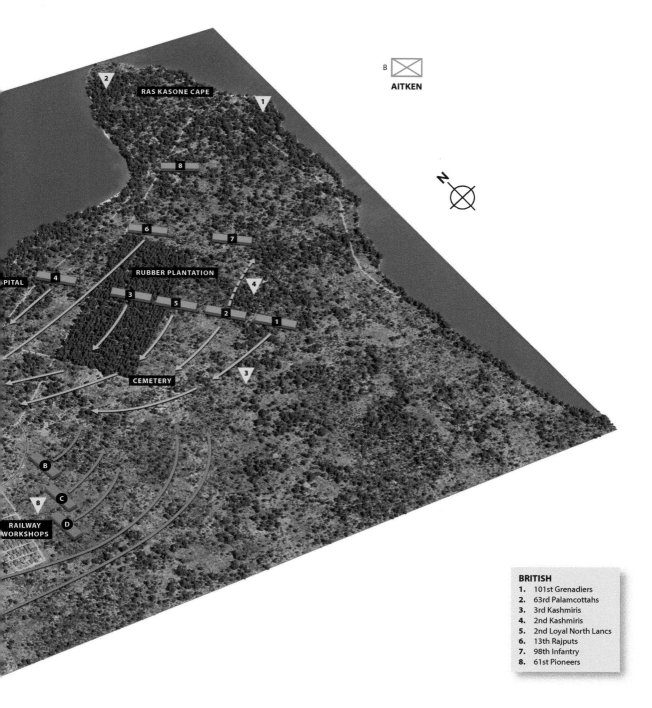

B ⊠

AITKEN

RAS KASONE CAPE

RUBBER PLANTATION

PITAL

CEMETERY

B

C

D

RAILWAY
WORKSHOPS

BRITISH
1. 101st Grenadiers
2. 63rd Palamcottahs
3. 3rd Kashmiris
4. 2nd Kashmiris
5. 2nd Loyal North Lancs
6. 13th Rajputs
7. 98th Infantry
8. 61st Pioneers

▽ EVENTS

1. The landings at Beach A on the night of 2–3 November fail to capture the town.

2. Landings at Beach B commence on the morning of 3 November, but no move inland is made until the following day.

3. The British line advances slowly and the engagement starts around 15:00hrs.

4. The 63rd Palamcottahs come under heavy machine-gun fire and some fall back.

5. Other elements of the British line continue to advance.

6. 6 FK is forced back by weight of numbers and street-fighting ensues.

7. Prince commits two of his companies, 7 and 8 SchK, to re-establish control of the town and the British units are pushed back.

8. Baumstark is also forced to commit his reserve force earlier than expected to check the overwhelming British advance.

9. Von Lettow delivers his 'right hook', unleashing 13 FK on the left flank of the British line.

10. The late-arriving 4 FK is hurled straight into the attack at 16:40hrs, landing another blow on the exposed British flank.

Indian troops taken prisoner during the fighting around Tanga. Badly led, they suffered a humiliating defeat at the hands of a far inferior force. (Photo by ullstein bild/ullstein bild via Getty Images)

the 13th Rajputs, pushed 6 FK back into the town itself and fierce street-fighting ensued. Prince, commanding the German reserve, took the decision to commit some of his men. It was earlier than von Lettow had planned, but it was unavoidable. Prince's *Schützenkompagnien* halted the British advance and gradually helped 6 FK push them back out of the town.

Baumstark had also committed men earlier than would have been hoped, with the weight of attacking troops almost irresistible. There was a moment where the German line almost cracked, but von Lettow and his fellow officers put on a show of disdain for the withering fire coming from the British. Actually laughing out loud, they convinced their men to hold fast, but the time had come to launch a counterattack if the day was to be saved.

Only one company remained, 13 FK, but it was one of von Lettow's best, and it had four machine guns. The German position, heavily outnumbered as they were, ought to have been hopeless, but Aitken's men were advancing on a compacted front which would barely outflank the Germans even if it held its initial course. The British left, the strong 101st Grenadiers, instead wheeled slightly to fill the gap left by the Palamcottahs, and this made them vulnerable to an attack on their own flank. This was where von Lettow unleashed 13 FK. He recalled: '… no witness will forget the moment when the machine-guns of the 13th Company opened a continuous fire at this point and completely reversed the situation.'

The 101st Grenadiers put up stubborn resistance, aided by two machine guns from the Palamcottahs that had not fled the field, but they were forced to pull back. The arrival of 4 FK, around 16:40hrs, effectively landed another right hook on the exposed chin of the British line. 'In wild disorder the enemy fled in dense masses, and our machine-guns, converging on them from front and flanks, mowed down whole companies to the last man,' wrote von Lettow. He was getting carried away in his report, but the British position was crumbling. The 98th had finally advanced, but too late to help the North Lancs and Kashmir troops being forced out of Tanga. In the failing light, the British withdrawal became general.

Von Lettow was not the sort of commander to let an enemy disengage easily, however, and he planned to pursue the British troops. Only a puzzling episode prevented the day from becoming even worse for Aitken's mauled army. A bugler sounded the recall to the German units, who interpreted it as a call to return to their base, outside Tanga. Before von Lettow realized what was happening, his small army had been spirited away and there was no opportunity to reorganize in time to turn the screw on the shattered invasion force.

For a brief period, then, Tanga was unoccupied once more, but Aitken did not have the imagination to grasp the gift. He set about bringing his force back on board the ships massed offshore, and the British invasion of German East Africa was over.

German losses over the two days of fighting amounted to 145, with 16 Germans and 48 *askari* and African carriers dead (among the dead was von Lettow's friend, Tom Prince). Aitken's losses were on an entirely different scale. No fewer than 817 casualties had been sustained, with 359 dead, 310 wounded and another 148 missing. Given the huge superiority of numbers enjoyed by Aitken, it was one of the most humiliating defeats in the history of the British Army.

Adding further to the humiliation, huge quantities of materiel were left behind on the beaches when the British departed. This included 16 machine guns, 455 rifles, 600,000 rounds of rifle ammunition, clothing, telephone equipment, coats and blankets. In all, there was enough to equip three German companies. In a war where resupply was going to be next to impossible, this was a windfall of huge proportions.

Von Lettow overestimated the British losses, believing he had killed at least 2,000 men, but he had scored a decisive blow, and one that would haunt the British. 'Years afterwards,' he recalled, 'I was asked by English officers whether we had used trained bees at Tanga.'

The Battle of Jasin

Following this devastating reversal, the British pulled their horns in. Aitken attempted to cast blame for the defeat on anybody but himself, but he was relieved of command on 4 December, after the confused story of the battle was fully comprehended back home. He was replaced by Brigadier-General Richard Wapshare, but it was Tighe who proved the more energetic general. The entire war effort in East Africa was being reconsidered back home, with the Colonial and India offices relinquishing control to the War Office.

Wapshare organized his command, with Tighe at Mombasa and Stewart at Bissil, giving them virtual autonomy in their respective areas. Under Tighe's leadership, British troops worked to stabilize their border with German East Africa – there was suddenly a very real possibility that the Germans might turn the tables and do a little invading of their own. At the same time, there was a directive from home not to undertake any offensive moves into German territory. As such, Tighe's operations in the Umba Valley, on the border, were acceptable. His subsequent taking of the village of Jasin, on Christmas Day, was not. Jasin was several miles inside German East Africa and the move was considered by von Lettow to be intolerably provocative.

The make-up of Tighe's force in these operations was significant for one particular detail. Alongside men of the 2nd Battalion Kashmir Rifles, 101st Grenadiers and 3rd Battalion Gwalior Infantry were two companies of the 3rd Battalion King's African Rifles. For the first time in the war, Britain was using native African troops offensively. There had previously been a ridiculous notion that Africans should be left out of any war on their own continent – pitting them against European enemies might put dangerous ideas into their heads, and the Germans had been looked at askance for their use of *askari* in the fighting so far.

Christmas had arrived, and the war seemed to have barely started, let alone finished. On the Rufiji Delta, the cornered *Königsberg* enjoyed an unusual festive period. Deep enough into the delta to be considered safe (the *Königsberg* had a considerably smaller draught than any of the British vessels that stood a chance against her in a fight, and so could get higher up the river), Captain Loof decided to give his men a proper Christmas, setting up tables onshore and distributing alcohol and cigarettes, as well as a variety of gifts sent in from around German East Africa. A grim form of humour played out between the British and Germans. British sailors floated lanterns on bases shaped like small coffins upriver, bearing the jaunty note, 'Try our Christmas pudding – large six inch – small size four point seven.' The pudding sizes referred to the guns of the biggest ships in the British squadron, which outmatched *Königsberg*'s own 4.1in. armament. The Germans had no appetite to sample these wares, but remained cheery; when the British sent a message via wireless a week later, the Germans were quick to reply. 'We wish you a happy New Year and hope to see you soon,' the British said. 'Thanks for the message,' the Germans responded. 'If you wish to see us we are always at home.'

Matters here, however, as on land, were slipping into a stalemate. The British did not have enough quality troops to achieve much, and overtures were already being made to South Africa, but for the time being they were tied up with operations of their own in German South-West Africa. Unable to accept just kicking their heels, the British looked for a suitably manageable target, and it was found off the Rufiji Delta.

The exotically named Mafia Island was not of much consequence, but it did offer the British a more convenient base from which to keep an eye on the *Königsberg*, and 500 men were dispatched to take it. This was accomplished with only a handful of casualties and Britain had another minor success with which to ease the embarrassment of Tanga.

Meanwhile, having driven up from Tanga to inspect the British positions at Jasin, von Lettow determined that an attack would provoke a response from the supporting encampments, and his plans included the laying of ambushes on the most likely routes for reinforcements to take. Calling his men in from New Moshi and Tanga, he assembled nine companies by 17 January and planned to attack the following day.

The German assault took the form of multiple columns converging on Jasin. A frontal assault was led by an unreliable 'Arab corps' (a rare flaw in von Lettow's planning that would have consequences), with 9 FK following. Two guns supported this column. Looping around to the right was Major

Kepler, with 11 and 4 FK, while Captain Adler swung around to the left with 15 and 17 FK. A strong reserve comprised 1, 6 and 13 FK, along with 7 SchK and the two ancient guns that had arrived too late to do much at Tanga.

A German machine-gun crew, with a light field piece also visible in the foreground. In this photo an *askari* is manning the gun, although it would have been more usual for a white NCO to perform this duty. (Public Domain)

The element of surprise was lost when the skittish Arab corps fired into the air and bolted (they were massacred by the German company following behind), and progress was slow over painfully difficult terrain. The fort had already fired off distress rockets before a shot was fired, and when action commenced in earnest, von Lettow was surprised by the volume of fire his men received. In his memoirs, he claimed that the presence of a fort was a complete surprise to him, describing it as 'strongly constructed and excellently concealed'. It is possible, in the thick coconut plantations, with sisal plants forming an undergrowth that was often difficult to push through, that he had simply missed it during his reconnaissance.

With the fort putting up stubborn resistance, the day deteriorated into a stalemate. The garrison, including over a hundred men from the 101st Grenadiers, KAR machine-gunners and Gurkhas, held out long enough for relief to come from Tighe's main camp at Umba. Unfortunately for them, Tighe was in no hurry to send reinforcements, and the few men that did try to come to the rescue were met by carefully placed German units. Von Lettow had once more demonstrated his ability to scout and plan ahead.

The battle continued into the night in intolerable heat, flaring up again the next morning until the garrison ran out of ammunition. Surrender followed and von Lettow had another victory, but at an appalling cost. Six German officers and 18 German NCOs had been killed out of a total of around 300 casualties. Von Lettow had lost another close friend, in the form of Captain von Hammerstein, shot while walking next to the German commander. A total of 200,000 rounds of ammunition had also been expended. It was a ruinously costly victory, and von Lettow was forced to accept that such offensive schemes would have to be shelved if he wasn't to break his small army in a series of such triumphs. Coupled with the directive from Lord Kitchener that the British were not to undertake any offensive operations, the stage was set for the second phase of the war.

PART II: THE RAILWAY WAR

The actions at Tanga and Jasin had shown von Lettow that he could take the British forces on and win, but he did not have the necessary resources to get drawn into a straight fight.

'We had to economize our force in order to last a long war,' he later recollected. 'The need to strike great blows only quite exceptionally, and to restrict myself principally to guerrilla warfare was evidently imperative.'

At the same time, von Lettow received devastating news from home. Private mail did not often get through, and on 12 February he received one of many letters sent by his sister, informing him that his brother had been killed on the Western Front nearly six months earlier. Diverting British resources from the fighting in Europe must suddenly have taken on a new poignancy for the German commander.

Reorganization of his forces was in order, and new units also needed to be raised. Over the course of 1915 von Lettow increased his *askari* numbers to around 12,000, with another 3,000 or so Europeans. It was the largest number of men he would command during the whole war (and would gradually be whittled away to even less than he had started the campaign with).

New troops appeared as if from nowhere. Throughout the year von Lettow became aware of more and more small units that had spontaneously formed throughout the territory. He amalgamated these into company-sized

The construction of the Uganda Railway had been a massive engineering project for the British, taking five years to complete. Its huge length made it extremely vulnerable to sabotage efforts. (Haeckel Brothers/Paul Thompson/FPG/Getty Images)

Damaging the railway, and destroying locomotives and rolling stock, proved considerably easier than building the railway in the first place, although the German troops employed had to be bold and resourceful in their work. (Public Domain)

formations, eventually fielding 60 companies. The shortage of Europeans or *askari* experienced enough to work as NCOs put a cap on any further expansion ('it would only have meant the creation of units without cohesion,' von Lettow explained).

Three corps were set up at the start of the year, commanded by Major Georg Kraut (north), Count Falkenstein (south-west) and Major (although von Lettow always referred to him as general) Kurt Wahle (west). This was an integrated army. The distinction between *Feldkompagnien* and *Schützenkompagnien* was blurred as von Lettow fed Europeans into his *askari* companies to replace those lost in battle. At the same time, *askari* were incorporated into the previously all-European units until, by the end of the year, company composition was the same whatever the unit's designation. In many instances, white troops took orders from African NCOs.

The Royal Navy's command of the ocean was manifesting itself in a strangling blockade, so von Lettow also had to tackle the less obviously warlike matters of replacing uniforms and boots, and the critical problem of a shortage of quinine. German scientists at the Amani Biological Institute in Usambara worked out a way of synthesizing this priceless drug, which was administered to European troops under the name of 'Lettow *schnapps*'.

British forces in East Africa may have been badly shaken, but they were still formidable through their sheer weight of numbers, so von Lettow turned his attention to a more vulnerable target – the Uganda Railway. Over the course of the year, raids would bring it to the point of total collapse.

It had taken the British almost five years to construct the 700-mile railway from Mombasa to Kisumu. The terrain had been all but impossible, and nature itself seemed determined to halt the enterprise at times, never more so than through the infamous 'Tsavo maneaters', a pair of unusually large lions that terrorized rail workers in 1898.

Von Lettow organized his campaign carefully, with different tactics for raids to the north and to the east. From bases in the foothills of Mount Kilimanjaro, his men set out northwards through the desert in teams of

Bridges were especially tempting targets, requiring huge amounts of work to repair. The use of pressure-activated fuses allowed a train to be taken down at the same time. (Public Domain)

around eight men, mixing *askari* with Europeans. The principal aim of these small parties was to prey on British patrols and columns, and the primary goals were rifles, ammunition and horses. One raid netted nearly 60 horses (prompting a British soldier captured during the raid to praise it as 'a damned good piece of work'), which contributed to the setting up of a second German mounted company. These companies allowed the campaign to operate on a bigger scale. The railway came into range and track, locomotives and bridges were targeted. Dynamite was easy to get hold of, and the Germans benefited from a large supply of demolition charges captured at Tanga.

Charges were placed on tracks, with pressure fuses to ensure the ensuing explosion would disable a train as well as tear up the track. The British countered by having a train push a couple of heavily laden wagons in front of it, hoping to trigger the charge and spare the locomotive, but the Germans quickly responded with delayed charges.

The Germans put 32 locomotives out of commission, while blowing up nine bridges between March and May. Great swathes of track were destroyed in this manner, conjuring images of the marauding troops of General Sherman, who tackled the rail network of Georgia on a much larger scale during the American Civil War.

When raiding to the east, von Lettow employed even smaller patrols, who would be out for up to two weeks at a time. The bush was thicker in this region, and progress was slow. The groups (a couple of Europeans, two or three *askari*, and a few carriers) needed to live off the land, although the time-honoured ritual of drinking your own urine was resorted to on numerous occasions.

As well as his small raiding parties, von Lettow also unleashed bands of up to 30 men aimed at hunting down and destroying the British patrols in the area. As well as preventing the British from interfering with the work of destroying the railway, these platoon-sized units (whose armament would include machine guns) also kept an eye open for opportunities to seize supplies and horses.

Such work was far from easy. The railroad may have been vulnerable, but the territory through which it snaked was inhospitable. The barren landscape, lack of water and wild animals made it a hair-raising endeavour. Fires could not be lit at night (denying the raiding parties comfort, cooked food and protection from wildlife) because mounted patrols sent out by the British were a constant threat. Everything depended on being able to move, with the result that extreme measures were often taken; a wounded comrade, unable to walk, might be left behind.

Casualties through the year were low, however. Only around 20 men were lost, making the campaign a signal success. Disaster was only narrowly averted on one occasion, however, when von Lettow himself accompanied a patrol that promptly lost its water supply.

Water, as always, was the critical commodity, and the British proved willing to bend the rules of war a little in this regard. Strictly forbidden from poisoning waterholes, the British instead took to merely posting warning signs, saying that a waterhole *had been* poisoned. A few animal carcasses, laid near the water but not actually in it, completed the illusion, and the ruse was enough to deter the Germans from using the holes in question.

The blockade runner *Rubens* brought a huge amount of supplies to von Lettow when it was run aground in early 1915. Her captain brought news of the fighting in Europe, which was almost as welcome as the ammunition and weapons. (Public Domain)

In April, German morale was boosted by the arrival of fresh supplies. A blockade runner, *Rubens*, had been run aground by her captain while being pursued by British ships, but remarkably the British had not destroyed her, allowing the bulk of the supplies she carried to be unloaded.

Ammunition had deteriorated in the saltwater, but by dismantling cartridges, drying the powder and making new ones, the Germans received a welcome boost to their stock of ammunition. Saving their best cartridges for the precious machine guns (kings of the battlefield in East Africa as on the Western Front), the less reliable salvaged cartridges were good enough for rifles. A misfire rate of 20 per cent was considered acceptable, and ammunition batches that did not perform at this standard were reserved for target practice.

The ship's commander, Lieutenant Christiansen, became a local celebrity, enthralling the Germans with tales from Europe and boosting morale further. 'The terrific fighting at home, the spirit of self-sacrifice and boundless enterprise which inspired the deeds of the German troops, awakened a response in our hearts,' von Lettow would remember. 'Many who had been despondent now took courage once more.'

All the time, British numbers were dwindling as a result of the harsh climate and tropical disease. It has been commented that von Lettow allowed nature to do much of the fighting for him, and it won a string of victories in 1915. Regiments that had arrived with IEFs B and C began to simply dissolve. Malaria and dysentery were the usual culprits, with the 13th Rajputs so ravaged by the end of the year that almost the entire regiment was withdrawn to recuperate.

Yellow fever, blackwater fever, sleeping sickness and 'relapsing fever' made up a gruesome list of options for newly arriving troops. If a soldier avoided these, he might fall to typhoid, cholera or 'croupous pneumonia'. Sleeping sickness epitomized the pitiless nature of the region. There were two kinds; one borne by flies that liked damp shade and one borne by flies that liked the hot sun. There was simply no escape.

Immunization had virtually eliminated smallpox in German East Africa and troops were routinely immunized against yellow fever, cholera and typhoid as well. In the German Army, as well as the essential mosquito nets, *askari* and porters would team up in the evening to check each other for ticks. The pesky fleas, known as 'jiggers', that enjoyed burrowing beneath toenails were particularly feared.

The British preference of bringing in foreign troops saw them suffer more than the native warriors in von Lettow's ranks. Indian regiments routinely had 20 per cent of their men on the sick list – and this was better than the norm (excellent camp discipline may have helped). When South African

A German column moves through the bush beneath a huge banyan tree, in this illustration by von Lettow's adjutant. (Public Domain)

troops came into the war, they averaged 50 per cent. As well as sapping the strength of the army, the scale of sickness was disastrous for the cohesion of units. Men were given almost no time to get used to serving together before a large proportion would be invalided out, and this had a particular effect on such things as gun teams, where smooth cooperation was vital.

'In this country, where sickness is so rife, it is impossible to keep an efficient gun team together for any length of time,' commented a British artilleryman. 'Old hands slip away each week, and men to replace them have endlessly to be instructed in the intricate mechanism of the gun.'

Maintaining sufficient troop numbers to mount a credible threat to the Germans required regular influxes of new men, but East Africa was way down on the list of priorities for the British, and reinforcements were limited. They included the 130th Baluchis and the 25th Battalion Royal Fusiliers (drawn largely from the colourfully named 'Legion of Frontiersmen', an irregular force).

Around the same time, a change in command at the head of the British Army in East Africa saw Tighe take over from Wapshare. Tighe had many qualities, but the patience necessary to effectively wait a year while reinforcements were summoned from South Africa was not one of them. Like an old war horse, he trembled at the prospect of battle, and his advancing alcoholism did not help matters. It is possible that by this stage he had started to suffer from hallucinations. Sitting on his backside was not his style – he would demand action.

The death of the Königsberg

Down on the Rufiji Delta, life was becoming increasingly difficult for the crew of the *Königsberg*. The ship's smaller guns had been removed and set up in riverside emplacements to attack any vessel attempting to get upstream, but while the British couldn't get in, she could not get out. At the peak of the operation, 24 ships kept the German light cruiser bottled up like a lion in a zoo.

Having limped into her refuge, with badly furred boilers that needed a port's facilities to scrape clean, *Königsberg* was now fighting fit. Unable to get to a port, the Germans had, almost miraculously, dismantled and removed her boilers and dragged them overland to Dar-es-Salaam, where they had been made spick and span once more. The return journey was quicker and the German ship had boilers as good as new, but no way of exercizing them.

Conditions were appalling for aerial operations, but getting a firm grasp on the *Königsberg*'s position was vital. A small landing strip was built on

Hunting the *Königsberg*

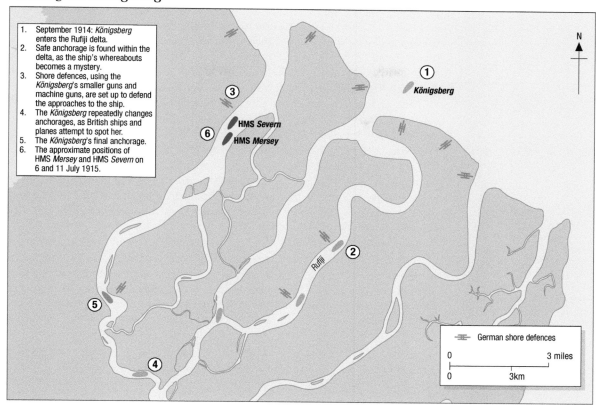

1. September 1914: *Königsberg* enters the Rufiji delta.
2. Safe anchorage is found within the delta, as the ship's whereabouts becomes a mystery.
3. Shore defences, using the *Königsberg*'s smaller guns and machine guns, are set up to defend the approaches to the ship.
4. The *Königsberg* repeatedly changes anchorages, as British ships and planes attempt to spot her.
5. The *Königsberg*'s final anchorage.
6. The approximate positions of HMS *Mersey* and HMS *Severn* on 6 and 11 July 1915.

① *Königsberg*

③

⑥ HMS *Severn*
HMS *Mersey*

② *Rufiji*

⑤

④

German shore defences

0   3 miles
0   3km

Mafia Island and pilots took their lives in their hands to try to catch a glimpse of the German cruiser as she paced up and down in her cage.

The *Kronborg*, sent to coal the *Königsberg* in hopes of facilitating a breakout, was sunk by HMS *Hyacinth* on 14 April, but once more the Germans were able to recover a huge amount of supplies, including medicine, five million rounds of ammunition, 2,000 rifles, a battery of light guns and four machine guns. The supplies would find their way to von Lettow, offering another priceless lifeline.

HMS *Mersey* was one of three monitors originally ordered by the Brazilian Navy, but Britain saw a use for the shallow-draught warships and held onto them. The *Mersey* and *Severn* played the key role in the hunt for the *Königsberg*.

On 25 April, the endgame opened when a flimsy Henry Farnum plane flew over the German cruiser and took a photograph on a Box Brownie camera. There were ideas that sturdier planes might be able to actually drop bombs on the German ship, but such dreams quietly faded. The British, however, had other pieces on their chessboard, and they moved two of them, the monitors *Mersey* and *Severn*, slowly and laboriously over 5,000 miles, from the Mediterranean to the mouth of the Rufiji.

One of the most colourful characters of the entire war now took centre stage, in the form of Piet Pretorius, a tracker, elephant hunter and former farmer who had been turfed out of his plantation on the Rufiji Delta by the Germans. Pretorius was a hard, uncompromising man, and his antagonism towards the Germans was a boon for the British, who set him to work charting the delta to get accurate measurements of the river's depth. The job took weeks, but Pretorius managed to get close enough to the German ship to provide valuable intelligence on her condition, winning the DSO for his efforts.

On the night of 5–6 July 1915, the two monitors glided into position to attack the *Königsberg*. Originally commissioned for the Brazilian Navy, their sumptuous fixtures and fittings had been ripped out, and with a draught of just six feet they could easily get within range of the German cruiser. The pair of 6in. guns on each monitor meant they were more than a match for the *Königsberg*.

The mangled wreckage of the *Königsberg*, following her scuttling. Half of her crew had already been commandeered by von Lettow prior to the ship's sinking, and the survivors now joined forces to continue their resistance to the British invasion on land. (Mondadori via Getty Images)

With help from planes spotting the fall of shells, the monitors engaged the German ship, but the day was inconclusive. Six hits were scored, but this was out of a total of 635 fired. The *Mersey*, meanwhile, had her fore gun knocked out of action. Loof lost five of his crewmen, with another 35 wounded, and one of his lieutenants, perhaps seeing no way out of the hellish situation, committed suicide following the day's action.

The 10 large guns rescued from the *Königsberg* continued to fight against British forces in East Africa for the remainder of the war. (Public Domain)

On 11 July, the monitors returned and this time the attack was more successful. The *Severn* found the *Königsberg*'s range and started to score regular hits, while Loof took a shrapnel wound that looked like it might be fatal. The conclusion to the encounter was inevitable, and at 14:00hrs, the *Königsberg* was scuttled using one of her own torpedoes. It had taken 252 days for the German ship to be destroyed – the longest naval engagement in history – and 33 of her crew were now dead. Not among that number was Loof himself, who survived through the time-honoured means of a pocket watch and cigarette case limiting the damage done by the shrapnel that had hit him in the stomach.

It was an ignoble end for a proud vessel, but the *Königsberg* would continue to fight. Her 4.1in. guns were recovered under the direction of Lieutenant-Commander Schoenfeld and continued to play a role in the war for the duration. Von Lettow was saddened by the demise of the ship, but welcomed the remainder of her crew and such stores as she had left.

The raid on Bukoba

Despite being under orders not to undertake any risky operations, Tighe was too belligerent to do nothing while his army dissolved around him. A large-scale offensive may have been off the table, but there were smaller targets to pick off without causing too much consternation back home – indeed, permission was granted by the War Office to launch a raid against the German radio mast at Bukoba, on Lake Victoria. British capabilities on the lake had perversely been boosted by the sinking of HMS *Pegasus*. Just as *Königsberg* would fight on in the form of her big guns, so too did *Pegasus* – her guns arming a motley collection of steamers on the lake, which could be used to offer fire support for the attack.

A recent influx of new troops gave Tighe enough manpower to throw at Bukoba, and he assembled a force of around 1,500 men, including 300 of the 2nd Battalion Loyal North Lancs, 400 men from the 25th Battalion Royal Fusiliers, 450 from the 3rd KAR and 200 from the 29th Punjabis. Two guns from the 28th Mountain Battery would supplement the guns of the Lake Victoria flotilla, and there was a total of eight machine guns. Against this, the Germans had about 200 *askari* in Bukoba, supported by three 75mm guns.

The attack, under Brigadier-General Stewart, was originally planned for the night of 20 June, but German sentries saw the brightly lit flotilla approaching and warning rockets were fired. Stewart therefore decided to

ATTACK ON THE *KÖNIGSBERG*, 11 JULY 1915 (PP. 46–47)

Five days after the *Königsberg* was first attacked by monitors in the Rufiji Delta, British ships returned to finish off the German light cruiser. Two spotter planes circled the cornered German ship, relaying information to the monitors.

Flying conditions were dangerous. There was heavy cloud and the fragile planes were also hunted by shrapnel bursts from the *Königsberg* and improvised anti-aircraft installations on shore (**1**). One of the spotter planes is shown just after taking a hit from a shrapnel shell. It would ditch in the Rufiji shortly afterwards, although both crew members survived (**2**).

Only half of the *Königsberg*'s guns could be brought to bear on the monitors, her port armament unable to join the battle, but this meant the German ship would not rattle through her reserves of precious ammunition too quickly. The starboard guns

(**3**) were soon firing in response to the shots of *Mersey* and *Severn*. *Mersey* opened fire first, her shots first flying over her target and then falling short. Massive craters were left on the beach from this and the bombardment five days earlier (**4**), testimony to the tremendous power of the 6in. guns of the British monitors.

In contrast to the inaccuracy of the first assault, both monitors were soon finding their target regularly and *Königsberg* was gradually worn down. Two of her starboard guns were knocked out of action (**5**) and the most intense period of fire then followed, as *Severn* scored nine hits out of 15 shells in a devastating 12-minute period.

Even after the German ship was scuttled, *Mersey* continued to fire for a further 45 minutes, using the great plume of smoke billowing forth from *Königsberg* as a marker.

HMS *Usoga* was pressed into service as a troop carrier as one of the ragtag collection of vessels used by the British to mount the raid on Bukoba. (Chronicle/Alamy)

wait until dawn before disembarking. A curious choice of landing ground (a small beach penned in by a steep cliff) proved lucky. The Germans had not thought it possible to scale the cliff and no defences were awaiting Stewart's men as they made their way to shore. In contrast, Bukoba was pounded by the combined guns of the flotilla. The German response was also hampered by the fact that a considerable number of their men (a majority, according to some reports) were out on patrol under their commander, von Stuemer.

A ridge of high ground dominating the town became the focus of the British force, with the Fusiliers leading the way. German *askari* were pushed back and by the end of the day the British had their base to assault the town on the following morning. It was an uncomfortable night, with freezing rain lashing the troops, but spirits were high after their success.

The rain continued into the following day as the assault resumed. German resistance was stiffened by the return of von Stuemer, but reduced by the knocking out of two of their 75mm guns. One of the Fusiliers recalled seeing a red cross above one of the gun emplacements, but this ruse apparently fooled nobody. German resistance had been brave, but as his men were pushed back into the town itself, von Stuemer bowed to inevitability and withdrew. Bukoba had been captured and the radio mast, described by some as looking a little like a miniature version of the Eiffel Tower, was brought down by the Faridkot Sappers and Miners from IEF B.

The relative ease of the operation would serve as a welcome morale boost for an army mired in inactivity. Only 30 casualties had been taken (the Germans had suffered around 50), but the success was marred by the looting of the town afterwards. One version of events claims that Lieutenant-Colonel D. P. Driscoll of the Fusiliers requested permission to loot Bukoba, but it is not in keeping with the man's character, and asking permission to act like barbarians is a strange thing to do. Whoever the actual culprits were, property was seized and destroyed and there were multiple incidents of rape. The Fusiliers, who carried the can for the appalling behaviour, were known as the 'Boozaliers' for some time afterwards.

Lieutenant-Colonel Daniel Patrick Driscoll had served at the head of the Driscoll Scouts during the Second Boer War. He raised the 25th Battalion of the Royal Fusiliers, formed mostly from the ranks of the Legion of Frontiersmen, in February 1915. (Hulton Archive/Getty Images)

It had been a small operation and a small victory, but the raid had also opened up the route for Belgian involvement in the war in Africa. The Belgians, however, were proving slow to act and Tighe was losing patience with their apparent unwillingness to bring pressure to bear on the Germans.

Von Lettow also regained the initiative with an assault on the British and Belgian troops at Saisi, on the Rhodesian border. Although the 450-strong garrison held out for a week against a force twice its size, it emphasized the fact that the Germans were shaping the war, exactly as von Lettow wanted. Fearing a British invasion from that direction, von Lettow's aggressive move put any such plans on hold, but the real impediment to a larger-scale involvement on the part of the Belgians was German control over Lake Tanganyika. Acting as the border between German East Africa and the Belgian Congo, it would need to be in friendly hands before large numbers of Belgian troops could contemplate crossing to take the offensive.

The Tanganyika Expedition

Belgian involvement in the war had become a point of friction. The Belgians were keen to take the offensive, but getting within striking distance was difficult given the presence of the large lakes in the western portion of German East Africa. There was the possibility of moving up through Northern Rhodesia (a move stymied by von Lettow's offensive on Saisi), or through the German territories of Rwanda and Burundi, but control of Lake Tanganyika was essential if the Germans weren't to threaten the Belgians with an attack from the rear.

Cooperation with the Belgians had seemed within reach early in the war. Under Commandant Josué Henry, they were eager to get underway, but crippled by a lack of supplies and materiel. Henry committed himself to helping protect the borders of Northern Rhodesia and Uganda, and he proposed an ambitious joint operation in March 1915, in which the Belgians would invade Rwanda and Burundi while the British attacked Mwanza. The plan had the potential to overwhelm German forces in the north-west of German East Africa, but cooperation between the allies began to break down at this point.

In London, there was growing suspicion about Belgium's motives in Africa. It was true that the Belgians wanted to grab hold of some German territory quickly, in case the war did not last long. Such gains would be useful bargaining chips at the negotiating table and it was reasonable for Belgium to have an eye on such pragmatic matters, but Britain began to feel they were acting solely in their own best interests. A new Belgian commander, General Tombeur, did nothing to ease these concerns as he immediately began to plan for an independent offensive.

An incursion into German territory from the west was vital to British plans, and thankfully the two allies were united in one aim – gaining control of Lake Tanganyika. The Germans had wrestled it from Belgian hands with the sinking of the *Alexandre Delcommune*, and their grip was about to be tightened by the launching of a new predator on the vast waters of the lake – the *Goetzen*. One of the great engineering feats of the war, the *Goetzen* had been built in Germany and then immediately broken up and transported to Dar-es-Salaam in 5,000 crates. From there she had made a piecemeal progress to Kigoma, on Lake Tanganyika, where she had been put back together like a Meccano set. The 220-foot-long steamer dominated the waters when she

was launched in June 1915. Shortly afterwards she was armed with one of the 4.1in. guns salvaged from the *Königsberg*.

One of the 4.1in. guns from the *Königsberg* found its way to Lake Tanganyika, where it made the *Goetzen* temporary master of the stretch of water that formed the border between the Belgian Congo and German East Africa. (Public Domain)

The solution to this was rather obvious, but no less remarkable for that. The British decided to bring their own boats to Lake Tanganyika to take on the *Goetzen*. These were not to be huge steamers, though, but small speedboats, heavily armed and specifically designed to both outpace and outgun the bigger German ship. The two boats chosen for the task, the 40-foot-long *Mimi* and *Toutou*, set off on their 10,000-mile journey from Great Britain under the watchful eye of the eccentric Lieutenant-Commander Geoffrey Basil Spicer-Simson. The last 3,000 miles of the trek would be overland from Cape Town, but the incredible feat was accomplished in less than four weeks. *Mimi* and *Toutou* were floated on the waters of Lake Tanganyika before Christmas 1915.

The two boats quickly set about tackling the smaller vessels in the German flotilla. *Kingami* was captured on 26 December and renamed *Fifi*. Now armed with an automatic 12-pound gun, *Fifi* turned on and sank her former comrade, *Hedwig*, on 8 February.

The Germans were aware that ships were going missing, but did not know how, and they were unwilling to send *Goetzen* out to investigate. For the time being, stalemate settled in on Lake Tanganyika, but a decisive intervention was awaited with some impatience. The Belgians were building a big cruiser of their own, the *Baron Dhanis*, but seemed to be in no hurry.

Salaita Hill

Massive South African reinforcements were on their way by the end of the year, and it wasn't a moment too soon. Three-quarters of the Indian troops that had made up IEFs B and C were either dead or sick by the end of 1915. The Loyal North Lancs had been reduced to 278 men fit for action, out of a starting point of 1,100. The first British attempt to wrest control of German East Africa had been frustrated by von Lettow, but the real damage had been done by East Africa itself.

New Indian troops were also arriving, of a higher quality than those in the expeditionary forces (the 129th Baluchis and 40th Pathans had gained experience on the Western Front), and a new commander-in-chief was on his way to replace Tighe. Horace Smith-Dorrien had experience of fighting in Europe and Africa, but he contracted pneumonia on his way to take command. He then hurried his recuperation and relapsed – his war in East Africa ended before it had started and another new commander was needed. A South African seemed the obvious solution, given the changing shape of the rebuilding British Army, and Jan Christian Smuts was finally settled on.

In the meantime, Tighe was unwilling to just sit and do nothing as a new army grew around him. His instincts were sound – the army would never be healthier than in its first few weeks in the field, and something might be achieved that would facilitate Smuts when he put together his plans for the coming campaign. Tighe therefore had good reasons for turning his sights on a hill that guarded the approach to German-held Taveta. This was the route into German East Africa and it would need to be cleared at some point. The British commander hoped for a quick, straightforward victory on the slopes of Salaita Hill. What he got was another humiliating defeat.

Von Lettow was aware of the large numbers of men flooding into British East Africa. Formations of a thousand or more were seen on manoeuvres – newly arrived South African troops being put through their paces in this new and unfamiliar territory.

The 129th Baluchis had performed well on the Western Front, none more so than Sepoy Khudadad Khan, who won a Victoria Cross for his bravery in resisting a German offensive almost immediately after reaching the front line. (British Library/Alamy)

As these units pushed closer to Salaita Hill (known as Oldorobo Mountain to the Germans), von Lettow saw an opportunity. The German commander welcomed the prospect of a British assault. His men on the hill would hold and he would deliver a counterattack, aiming to secure a major victory.

A total of 6,000 troops was massed by Tighe for the assault, including the 2nd South African Infantry Brigade and the 1st East African Infantry Brigade. Commanded by Brigadier-General Wilfrid Malleson, the powerful force bristled with 41 machine guns and 18 field guns, and a lengthy artillery bombardment was to 'soften up' the enemy before the infantry went in. Two armoured cars added a novel and, ultimately, useful element to the battlefield. Something less than 1,000 Germans waited patiently on the slopes of the hill, dug in and prepared, with two guns of their own and 12 well-positioned machine guns.

Spotter planes gave the British clear sight of the German trenches and the artillery bombardment opened at 09:00hrs on 12 February, with two guns rescued from HMS *Pegasus* (affectionately known as 'Peggies') taking part. A familiar impression was created by the bombardment – surely nobody could survive such a pummelling, and the infantry was consequently ordered forward. South African troops advanced on the flank

The Assault on Salaita Hill, 12 February 1916

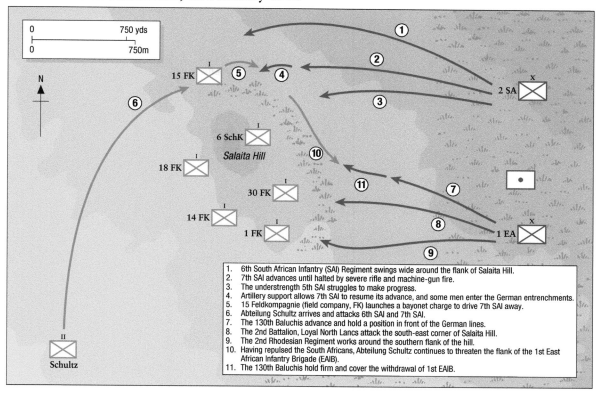

0   750 yds
0   750m

N

15 FK ⑤ ④
2 SA ✕
6 SchK
Salaita Hill ⑩
18 FK
30 FK ⑪ ⑦
14 FK
1 FK ⑧ 1 EA ✕
⑨

II
Schultz

1. 6th South African Infantry (SAI) Regiment swings wide around the flank of Salaita Hill.
2. 7th SAI advances until halted by severe rifle and machine-gun fire.
3. The understrength 5th SAI struggles to make progress.
4. Artillery support allows 7th SAI to resume its advance, and some men enter the German entrenchments.
5. 15 Feldkompagnie (field company, FK) launches a bayonet charge to drive 7th SAI away.
6. Abteilung Schultz arrives and attacks 6th SAI and 7th SAI.
7. The 130th Baluchis advance and hold a position in front of the German lines.
8. The 2nd Battalion, Loyal North Lancs attack the south-east corner of Salaita Hill.
9. The 2nd Rhodesian Regiment works around the southern flank of the hill.
10. Having repulsed the South Africans, Abteilung Schultz continues to threaten the flank of the 1st East African Infantry Brigade (EAIB).
11. The 130th Baluchis hold firm and cover the withdrawal of 1st EAIB.

of the German trenches, while the British, Indian and Rhodesian troops of the 1st East African Infantry Brigade (EAIB) took them head-on. Forcing their way through the thick scrub, the troops were already tired when they reached an ominous stretch of cleared ground, still 1,000 yards from the German lines. The troops pushed on, bravely, but were soon caught in heavy fire from the German positions. The apparent line of trenches, spotted from the air and subjected to the intense bombardment, was actually a dummy, empty of troops. The true German lines were lower down the hill, well covered by scrub. The South Africans were repulsed twice but managed to get some men into the German lines, before they broke when the Germans charged them with bayonets. The men of the 1st EAIB, rather than launching a diversionary attack at the same time, were not ordered forward until 10:45hrs, and quickly became pinned by German fire after entering the same cleared ground that had stalled the South Africans. By 12:00hrs it was clear the South Africans were in serious trouble, and the 1st EAIB was first ordered northwards to support them, and then ordered to attack the hill directly. Advancing proved impossible, however, although the men retired in better order than the South Africans had managed and the rout anticipated by von Lettow did not materialize when the 130th Baluchis stood firm against a German bayonet charge. Even so, it took a cool fighting retreat, lasting until 18:15hrs, to finally end the day with the British force still intact.

The 130th Baluchis recovered much of the equipment dropped by the scattered South Africans, especially satisfying considering the demeaning

THE ASSAULT ON SALAITA HILL (PP. 54–55)

The 2nd South African Infantry Brigade gave General Tighe fresh troops to throw at von Lettow-Vorbeck's *askari,* and they were given minimal time to acclimatize before being thrust into action. As a result they were fighting fit, but unused to the rigours of the theatre. Many of the men were also inexperienced and for some this would be their first taste of combat. Pictured are men of the 5th South African Infantry Regiment (**1**), still in their regulation light blue and white shirts (before long they would almost universally have switched to khaki shirts).

The plan of attack held some merit – it was intended that the brigade should outflank the German positions, swinging wide to the north of the hill and then attacking from the north-west. In the event, they strayed from this planned route and elements became engaged in a frontal assault. 5th SAI was also depleted to the tune of two companies prior to the attack, which were used to form a reserve.

With 6th and 7th SAI advancing to their right, 5th SAI, identified by their green and white helmet flashes, moved forward and came under sporadic fire from German artillery. However, it was the German machine guns (**2**), well placed along the base of the hill, that would do the real damage. One such gun, apparently mounted on the back of a mule, proved particularly troublesome until an armoured car (**3**) flushed it from its hiding place. Amid the confusion of the battle, von Lettow dismissed accounts from his men of *kifaru* (rhinos) moving through the bush, but their impact was very real.

With the preparatory British artillery barrage having mistakenly targeted a line of fake entrenchments closer to the top of the hill (**4**), the German machine-gun positions and artillery coordinated from two German command posts atop the hill (**5**) were able to operate with near impunity.

manner in which the South Africans had treated the Indian troops. The rescued equipment was returned with a polite note: 'With the compliments of the 130th Baluchis. May we request that you do not any longer refer to our sepoys as coolies.'

The 2nd SAIB lost 138 dead, with the 1st EAIB adding 34 more. It was not a large number, but the decisiveness of the defeat was yet another blow to British prestige. Tighe's instincts may have been correct, but his planning had proved woefully inadequate. As if passing judgement on the performance of the British officer class up to this point, the war was about to be handed over to the South Africans.

PART III: THE SOUTH AFRICAN OFFENSIVE

Jan Smuts had no intention of dancing to von Lettow-Vorbeck's tune. The South African general had very definite ideas of how to deal with the elusive German commander, and how to end the war in East Africa. As well as learning his trade in the Boer War, Smuts was also familiar with the Zulus, and he planned to enact their battlefield tactics on a grand scale.

Zulu *impis* traditionally approached in a large central body, grabbing and holding the attention of the enemy while they were enveloped by twin 'horns' moving around both flanks. Smuts believed this was the approach needed to finally deal with von Lettow. He planned to fix the German Army in place with a frontal assault, while flanking columns got behind it. In theory, there was some merit to this plan, but it would stand or fall on von Lettow's willingness to play his role.

As the build-up of men continued, Smuts could have no complaints over the resources at his disposal. He had around 27,350 men in British East Africa, as well as nearly 2,000 in Uganda and 2,500 in Northern Rhodesia. The Belgians had around 12,500 if they could be brought into the equation, giving the allies more than 40,000 men. There were no doubts about where

A German machine-gun position waits for the British to make their move on the border between German East Africa and British East Africa. (ullstein bild via Getty Images)

The 1916 offensive

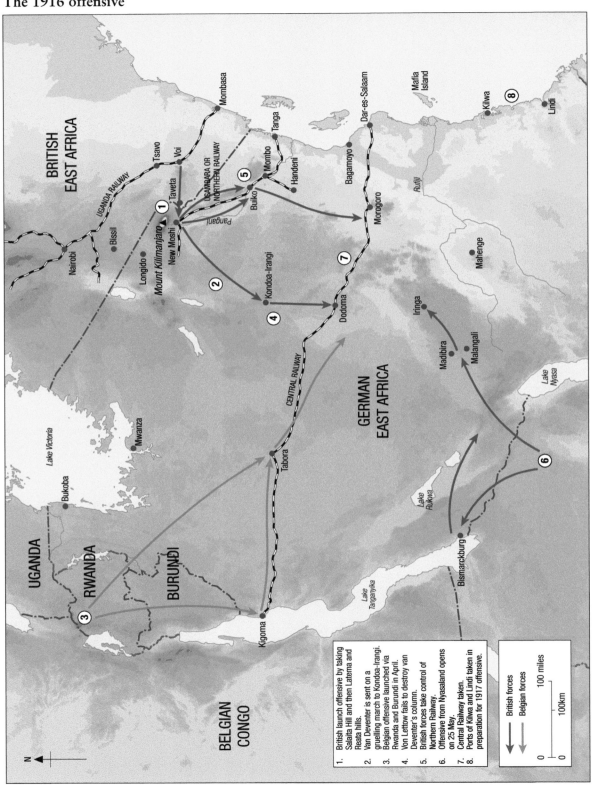

BRITISH EAST AFRICA

GERMAN EAST AFRICA

BELGIAN CONGO

UGANDA

RWANDA

BURUNDI

Mombasa

Tsavo

Voi

Taveta

Mount Kilimanjaro

New Moshi

Nairobi

Bissil

Longido

Buiko

Mombo

Tanga

Handeni

Bagamoyo

Dar-es-Salaam

Mafia Island

Kilwa

Lindi

Morogoro

Mahenge

Kondoa-Irangi

Dodoma

Iringa

Madibira

Malangali

Bismarckburg

Tabora

Kigoma

Mwanza

Bukoba

Lake Victoria

Lake Nyasa

Lake Rukwa

Lake Tanganyika

UGANDA RAILWAY

USAMBARA OR NORTHERN RAILWAY

CENTRAL RAILWAY

Pangani

Rufiji

1. British launch offensive by taking Salaita Hill and then Latema and Reata hills.
2. Van Deventer is sent on a gruelling march to Kondoa-Irangi.
3. Belgian offensive launched via Rwanda and Burundi in April.
4. Von Lettow fails to destroy van Deventer's column.
5. British forces take control of Northern Railway.
6. Offensive from Nyasaland opens on 25 May.
7. Central Railway taken.
8. Ports of Kilwa and Lindi taken in preparation for 1917 offensive.

British forces
Belgian forces

0   100 miles
0   100km

N

58

the rapidly expanding army was going – on 26 February, the 2nd Loyal North Lancs recorded being given a new set of maps of German East Africa.

Although they dwarfed von Lettow's army, the allied forces were scattered and the area available to the Germans to fall back into was simply vast. The failure to take Salaita Hill meant there was work to be done before the offensive could open in earnest, but the rainy season was due to start in a week or so. Smuts decided to chance his arm and set himself up with a launchpad for the major offensive he had in mind for after the rains had ended. Salaita Hill needed to be taken, and then twin positions at Reata and Latema hills, which dominated the road leading to Taveta, needed to be dealt with. Meanwhile, General Stewart, with the 1st Division, was ordered to proceed to New Moshi. Setting out on 5 March, he made good progress at first, but bogged down as his men became exhausted.

The second assault on Salaita Hill was an anti-climax. Tighe bombarded the position for some time before realizing it had been abandoned by the Germans, and the army moved forward to tackle Reata and Latema. The hills were imposing, being around 700 feet high, and the memory of Salaita Hill was still fresh. Commanded by Major Kraut, a thousand *askari* occupied the hills. Initially three companies held the line, with two in reserve, but all five companies were committed soon after the action began.

General Malleson was chosen to lead the assault but shortly after his troops ran into difficulties, he left the battlefield, citing illness. Tighe took over, but the assault was another costly shambles. Again opting for frontal attacks, 1,500 men of the 2nd Rhodesians, 3rd KAR and 130th Baluchis moved forward until compelled to find cover by the German machine guns. Tighe threw in reserves as soon as he got up to speed with the events of the day after taking over from Malleson, but progress was slow. Artillery helped the British force to advance up the deadly slopes, but the Baluchis eventually had to dig in on Latema, while the Rhodesians and KAR troops were sent reeling by a bayonet charge on Reata. Captain Koehl, commanding the two reserve companies of German *askari*, had intended to bring his men into action on the British flank, which may have proved devastating, but the denseness of the bush made such a manoeuvre unfeasible – it wasn't only the British who found themselves frustrated by the terrain on which they were forced to fight.

Von Lettow (left) alongside one of his most able commanders, Major Georg Kraut. (Public Domain)

Night fell and the situation became even more confused. At the German HQ, in New Moshi, von Lettow was kept apprised of the situation, as far as anyone could tell what the situation was. He was also alerted to the movements of a large body of mounted men, clearly aiming at outflanking the German position. The mounted South Africans, commanded by van Deventer, were making slow progress and suffering from heat, lack of water and the foolish decision to eat unripe bananas as they passed through a plantation. Von Lettow would claim that he planned to attack this column, whereas other interpretations insist he was spooked by having

mounted soldiers on his flank and overestimated the threat posed by van Deventer's exhausted men.

Rushing to the battlefront, von Lettow was there to see a night-time attack by the 5th and 7th South African Infantry regiments (sent after a request from Tighe for reinforcements) come unstuck. Having struggled to know where they were going in the dark, after moonrise they had advanced into the teeth of the German machine-gun positions.

The next morning, British troops rose from their dug-in positions and advanced up the hills once more, to find that the Germans had withdrawn. Von Lettow would later recognize this as a missed opportunity, but he had delivered another stinging rebuke to the British, who had suffered around 270 casualties.

It had been chaotic, and far from easy, but the road to New Moshi was now open, and the invasion of German East Africa could begin in earnest. How much of a role the 2nd Battalion Loyal North Lancs would play in that invasion, however, was uncertain. Following Salaita, they were down to 556 officers and men, and as well as regularly appearing in the thick of the action, illness was taking a steady toll, with the battalion's war diary regularly noting the passing of soldiers, usually due to dysentery. On 1 April 1916, the diary noted '110 men reported sick this morning. Whole Battn looks very ill.'

The next day, the battalion was informed of its place in the 1st East African Brigade for the invasion of German East Africa, but two days later 28 men were admitted to hospital with malaria and a steady stream were stricken from that point on. Major-General Arthur Reginald Hoskins, commanding the 1st Division, came to visit the next day, concerned at the erosion of one of his best units, and the possibility of the battalion being removed from active duty and sent to a healthier climate was first floated. By 19 April, a further 92 men had been hospitalized, and a letter to Lieutenant-Colonel O'Grady at headquarters suggested that the remaining healthy soldiers be used to bring the machine-gun and mounted companies up to full strength, with the remnants of the battalion shipped out to recuperate. By

24 April, 320 men were slated to travel to Egypt, while 167 would join the machine-gun company. The East African campaign could chew up battalions perfectly well without any assistance from the Germans.

Kondoa-Irangi

The rainy season was overdue as Smuts pondered his next move. Large-scale operations would be impossible once the rains started in earnest, but he was still tempted to set his plans in motion. It also appears that he underestimated the severity of the weather that was on its way, and may have been lulled by inaccurate reports from Boers who had settled in East Africa. His first task was to get rid of his under-performing generals, with Stewart and Malleson unceremoniously dispatched, while Tighe was treated with a little more respect – the man at least had an appetite for the fight.

Smuts was set on outflanking his opponent. His main move would be along the Northern Railway, where von Lettow had men in strength, but nothing could be done until after the rains. However, he believed it was worth the gamble to send van Deventer and the 2nd Division of his reorganized army on a flanking march. Consequently, he set van Deventer a daunting task. He was ordered to strike south-west to Kondoa-Irangi, where von Lettow had been gathering men. A strong German garrison could hold up the advance on the Central Railway, and Smuts felt he was in a race to get men to the region in strength.

It would not have been an easy march (covering 250 miles) even without the rains. Consulting local sources, Smuts had been informed that average annual rainfall in the Kondoa-Irangi region was just 3.5in., which did not sound like anything to be worried about. The problem was, this was wildly inaccurate intelligence.

Van Deventer duly set off with his 1st South African Mounted Brigade, about 1,200-strong, on the evening of 8 April. The 3rd South African Infantry Brigade and artillery units would follow and eventually catch up with him at Kondoa-Irangi. Progress was initially smooth, but van Deventer was leading his men into a nightmare. The area they were marching into was squarely in the tsetse fly belt. After two weeks, three-quarters of the column's horses were dead, and the rain was coming down in torrents. Smuts may have been feeling a twinge of foreboding when he noted, 'I have never in all my life dreamed that rain could fall as it does here,' but he had been assured that the rains were not as dramatic further south. The infantry and artillery slogging along after van Deventer had an even harder time, but at least they knew they were on the right track. All they had to do was follow the line of dead horses.

On 20 April, van Deventer's ragged column reached Kondoa-Irangi and the infantry and artillery trudged in 10 days later. A combined force of 10,000 had been reduced to 3,000 men fit for duty. 1,500 dead horses and mules were rotting along the route they had taken. Van Deventer's situation was perilous in the

A posed photograph of scouts advancing through the bush. Great care had to be taken not to run into an enemy ambush or fall foul of snipers. (The Print Collector/Getty Images)

A *Königsberg* gun mounted on a carriage. This heavy artillery helped von Lettow's forces pack a punch way above their weight. (The Protected Art Archive/Alamy)

extreme – his men were in no state to move out and secure the surrounding area, and von Lettow was therefore able to take up a strong position on hills four miles to the south.

The Germans had been boosted by the arrival of another blockade-runner. The *Marie* had slipped into Sudi Bay, packed to the gunnels with 1,500 tons of war materiel. It had taken more than a week for the ship to be unloaded and the treasure trove included four 105mm howitzers, 2,000 rifles with three million rounds of ammunition, a pair of 75mm mountain guns and thousands of shells for the guns recovered from the *Königsberg*, along with food, medicine, uniforms and even medals. Von Lettow himself received the Iron Cross, First and Second Class.

This was to be the last time the German Army received any supplies from the outside world, but such was the scale of the shipment, von Lettow was able to turn his thoughts to an offensive. Van Deventer's men, languishing in Kondoa-Irangi, presented an irresistible target.

Von Lettow had been stripping the Northern Railway of men, where they were not currently needed, and moving them to the Kondoa-Irangi region, gradually concentrating his force as South African numbers moved in the opposite direction due to disease. By 7 May, von Lettow enjoyed numerical superiority in terms of men fit for duty, having amassed 4,000 *askari*.

His two heaviest guns, a 3.5in. naval gun and a 4.1in. *Königsberg* gun, made life a misery for the South Africans, and he quickly forced their forward camps to fall back. Van Deventer had two *Pegasus* guns with him, and for a while a naval duel took place more than 200 miles from the ocean.

The Germans were not immune to the rain, and no attack on the South African position was remotely possible until the rains ended. Von Lettow pencilled in 10 May and waited. In the meantime, he determined to occupy the former advanced positions of the South Africans. Back at his headquarters, on the evening of 9 May, the German commander sought to wake himself up 'with a cup of coffee and a little rum', but the rum won out over the caffeine and he fell asleep. He was awoken to the news that fighting had erupted on the outskirts of Kondoa.

German units moving into their new positions had been surprised by a South African patrol and a battle had blown up. A serious German attack found that the South Africans had learned their lesson at Salaita – they had prepared a dummy line of entrenchments and were able to easily fend off multiple charges from stronger positions above and behind them.

Von Lettow listened helplessly: '... owing to the great distance, and the bushy and rocky country that would have to be traversed, I did not think I could engage the reserves I still had in hand with any prospect of success,' he recalled. 'It would take hours to obtain even the roughest idea of the situation, and the moon would be up for barely an hour more. For well or ill, therefore, I had to leave the fight in front to take its course.'

The battle's course was chaotic, as would be expected from a night-time encounter that had been planned by neither side. Von Lettow lost two German officers (Captain von Kornatzky and Lieutenant-Colonel von Bock) and over 100 *askari*. The 11th South African Infantry had borne the brunt of the attack, keeping the German *askari* at bay and drawing praise from von Lettow.

Despite the small-scale nature of the action, von Lettow observed the South Africans strengthening their defensive works over the coming days and reluctantly concluded that his great opportunity had passed. Still, there was an opportunity to make the South Africans' lives truly miserable. With two howitzers, a pair of mountain guns and the two naval pieces, von Lettow sent what van Deventer's men came to refer to as their 'daily hate', random shells lobbed into the town of Kondoa and the outlying positions. The favour was returned, but von Lettow spoke lightly of the 'nuisance... to have [the enemy's] heavy shell pitching into our camp every now and then.'

The Germans were also able to make better use of the surrounding countryside. While the South Africans struggled on meagre rations, von

Torrential rains could turn roads into rivers, making it almost impossible to make use of motorized transport. In better conditions, the Ford motor car earned rave reviews for its agility and sturdiness. (Public Domain)

Lettow seemed to be in high spirits when speaking of the bounty available. The main crop of the area being the millet-like *mtema*, his men dried it and ground it into flour, mixing it with wheat flour to make what von Lettow described as bread of 'really excellent quality'. There was also sugar cane, yams, peas and plentiful cattle. In short, 'in this extremely rich Kondoa country the troops could obtain a variety of food in abundance'. Their experience of the stalemate was very different to that of van Deventer's men.

The allies

One of the consequences of von Lettow concentrating forces at Kondoa-Irangi was the weakening of garrisons elsewhere. It was the inevitable consequence of working with such limited means, and had he secured the major victory that seemed within his grasp it would have been well worth it, but as the opportunity to destroy van Deventer's tattered division slipped through the German commander's fingers, the weakening of other areas had a telling effect.

To the north-west, three companies had been stripped from the force of Captain Max Wintgens. Wintgens' men had been tormenting the Belgians since the start of the war, holding firm in Rwanda and deterring any incursion. Now, Belgian ambitions coincided with the withdrawal of German troops, resulting in rapid advances into German East Africa at the same time that van Deventer's men were reaching Kondoa.

Wintgens had just 600 *askari* and 55 Europeans to hold Rwanda, while Major von Langenn-Steinkeller had less than 400 men to hold Burundi. Belgian forces had taken Rwanda by 21 May and Burundi was theirs less than a month later.

A Short Seaplane, similar to the type that photographed the *Goetzen* on Lake Tanganyika, taken from *The Wonder Book of Aircraft for Boys and Girls*. (Print Collector/Getty Images)

The German garrison at Kigoma, to the south, was even smaller but was hugely significant. Nestled on the shoreline of Lake Tanganyika, Kigoma was the base for the *Goetzen*, and the British and Belgians were not yet finished with her. The arrival of *Mimi* and *Toutou* had given the British *de facto* control of the lake, but the *Goetzen* was still a worrying presence. Spicer-Simson had been absent for a couple of months, scouting around for a vessel able to tackle the *Goetzen* head-on, and he had returned on 12 May with good news. The British Consul's personal ship, the *George*, was nearly three times the size of *Mimi* and *Toutou*, but almost as fast. Under Spicer-Simson's instructions, the ship had been appropriated, dismantled, and was being carried to Lake Tanganyika, where she would challenge the *Goetzen*.

Anglo-Belgian relations remained strained, with deep suspicions over the Belgians' sudden energy and enthusiasm for taking territory. On the lake, however, cooperation extended to the British providing the Belgians with four Short Type 827 seaplanes. Lake Tanganyika was not suitable for seaplane use, but Lake Tungwe was,

German *askari* at Dar-es-Salaam pose playfully for the camera. (Hulton-Deutsch Collection/CORBIS/Corbis via Getty Images)

although it was debateable how sensible it was to attempt to fly a plane from a base 2,500 feet above sea level, with a target 80 miles away.

Nevertheless, the Short Type 827s were used to hurl a few small bombs in the *Goetzen*'s general direction and later took useful aerial photographs, in a scene reminiscent of the *Königsberg*'s last days. Unbeknown to the Belgians, the *Goetzen*'s teeth had been pulled. Her 4.1in. *Königsberg* gun had been replaced by a dummy, the real thing having been sent to von Lettow. The *Goetzen*, once the scourge of Lake Tanganyika, was scuttled when the Germans abandoned their base at Kigoma.

Portuguese contributions to the war had been on a more limited scale than the Belgians'. With Portugal neutral into 1916, there had been little to fear from their corner, and von Lettow had petitioned Schnee to allow him to withdraw the single *Schutztruppe* company keeping an eye on the border with Portuguese East Africa (Schnee, fearing native unrest, had refused).

Multiple expeditionary forces were sent out to East Africa from Portugal. The first, numbering 1,527 men, arrived in November 1914, but it received no orders until May of the following year, by which point it barely existed anymore. A second expeditionary force of almost exactly the same size arrived in November 1915 and actually took the field the following April, after Germany had declared war on Portugal in March 1916. A force of 400 men advanced from Palma and captured Kionga easily, but an attempt to cross the Rovuma River in May was savaged by German machine-gun positions. Less than a month later, the Second Expeditionary Force was finished, having suffered staggering losses due to disease. The 21st Infantry Regiment, for example, had 102 dead and 600 sick or missing from its initial complement of 1,000 men. Only 19 of the casualties were from combat.

By the time Portugal sent its third expeditionary force, it was taking matters rather more seriously, and 6,000 men arrived in July 1916. Despite the fate met by the first two such forces, the Portuguese authorities seemed confident about what this new influx of men could achieve. The commanding officer, General Ferreira Gil, was under intense pressure both from his superiors back home and Smuts to the north. He was exhorted by both parties to begin an offensive quickly – but his men had already started to succumb to tropical diseases. The soldiers sent out from Portugal to East Africa became known, with good reason, as 'the condemned'.

The Northern Railway

As well as weakening German positions in the north-west, von Lettow's sucking in of troops to Kondoa-Irangi reduced numbers available to resist General Smuts' move along the Northern Railway when operations were able to start up again.

As was his usual style, Smuts planned an advance on a wide front. With men from his remaining two divisions, he formed three columns. Hoskins skirted the Pare Mountains with KAR units, Brigadier-General J. A. Hannyngton moved along the railway line and Brigadier-General S. H. Sheppard along the Pangani River. Mombo was the initial goal, and the offensive restarted on 18 May.

The enforced delay had been hard on Smuts' men. They had encamped in unhealthy territory and 2,000 South Africans were in hospital with various ailments. Still, he was putting 7,500 troops in motion and expectations were once more high. Awaiting them on the Northern Railway was Kraut, with just 2,000 men.

Smuts' instincts were to move quickly, but he repeatedly had to wait for his supply line to catch up with him. One such stop came on 30 May, at Buiko. The columns had been making reasonable progress, covering 100 miles, but it was nothing like the speed that would be needed to catch the German *askari*. Unless the Germans miscalculated, they would be like a bantamweight in the ring with a heavyweight, continuously dancing out of reach of their larger but slower-moving adversary. The bantamweight could land punches as well, and surprisingly heavy ones. Kraut had a *Königsberg* gun mounted on a railway carriage, meaning he could move it into range, fire at the advancing columns, and then swiftly move it away again. Improvized explosive devices, many of which were designed by a Dutch sailor from the blockade-runner *Rubens*, were also employed.

The capture of Mombo forced the Germans to abandon the Northern Railway, fearful of being cut off from their line of retreat via Handeni. A tramline ran from Mombo to Handeni and the Germans headed down this, while the single company in Tanga also moved out. The Northern Railway belonged to the British and Smuts' men captured Handeni on 19 June.

Five days later, von Lettow had finally had enough of the stalemate around Kondoa and quietly withdrew from his positions. His withdrawal was unchallenged, as van Deventer's men were still in an exhausted state. It would not be until the end of July that they were able to take Dodoma, on the Central Railway, just 100 miles to the south of their position.

On 7 July, Tanga itself finally fell into British hands. Despite its garrison having withdrawn, the town was subjected to a naval bombardment lasting nine hours, as if in retribution for the humiliation it had imposed on the British almost two years earlier. Smuts called another halt, east of the Nguru Mountains, after a six-week advance that had brought his men to the point of exhaustion. Only 250 miles had been covered.

Nevertheless, the German positions appeared to be unravelling as pressure was applied everywhere. Reports came in to von Lettow of his enemies advancing on all fronts. As well as the efforts of the Belgians, Portuguese and Smuts' main army, to the south-west an incursion was being made by yet another large body of troops.

Norforce

Brigadier-General E. Northey commanded a 2,600-strong force, operating out of Nyasaland. His men were a mixture of British South African Police, Northern Rhodesia Police, South African Rifles and King's African Rifles, and went under the name of 'Norforce'.

His move into the south-west corner of German East Africa was timed to coincide with the offensive movements elsewhere, in order to put maximum strain on von Lettow's resources. Splitting his men into four columns (Colonel Hawthorn commanding 800 men, Colonel Rodger 600, Major Flindt 400 and Colonel Murray 800), they moved into German East Africa on 25 May. The ultimate goal was to link up with van Deventer's men once they had pushed through to the Central Railway, but the destination was only part of the plan. En route, it was intended to destroy German forces in the area, believed to number around 1,500 (the number was actually considerably lower than this).

Murray's column got things off to an uncertain start, allowing the garrison of Namema fort to escape. Incensed, Murray then hared off after the withdrawing Germans, chasing them as far as Bismarkburg on Lake Tanganyika, despite energetic protestations from Northey.

On Northey's right wing, three further columns all failed to capture the garrisons of the German border forts they attacked. Despite this disappointment, Northey was able to bring his disparate columns together to tackle German positions at Malangali and Madibira on 24 July. Here, the Germans were expected to make a stand.

The smaller of the two enemy forces, around 200 *askari* at Malangali, was targeted, and an artillery duel ensued until the Germans were forced to withdraw after darkness fell. Now outflanked, the larger German force at Madibira, some 800 strong, also withdrew.

Northey's next move was on to Iringa, where he hoped to link up with van Deventer's force, just stirring from their long and uncomfortable visit to Kondoa. The Germans had moved away from their positions threatening van Deventer on 24 June, and von Lettow was faced with a dilemma. His overall strategy was working – he was tying down large numbers of enemy troops – but his options were dwindling. 'For an attack, the situation was altogether too unfavourable,' he admitted in his memoirs. 'The problem, therefore, was what should be the general direction of our retreat?'

He opted for the Mahenge region, where he was sure he could find enough food for his men, and where further retreat to the south would be possible if and when he was pressed again. Recognizing that Smuts was the most serious of the threats he faced, he pulled the bulk of his men back to Dodoma, then moved eastwards by rail to Morogoro. Kraut was doing the best he could to slow up Smuts' advance, but he was steadily being pushed back. Reinforcements would stiffen his resistance to the inexorable move towards the Central Railway.

Edward Northey, the energetic, driving commander of 'Norforce', had originally seen action on the Western Front, where he was wounded. He later served as the Governor of Kenya. (Public Domain)

Smuts' position, stalled once more as he waited for his supply lines to reach him, was bleak. His men were exhausted and the latest camp he had chosen was within range of the Germans' big guns. More 'daily hate' was delivered, but simply moving out of range did not seem to occur to the South African general, who stayed put for a month before resuming his advance. His move through the Nguru Mountains, however, was decisive and the Germans fell back time and time again – so much so that the German commander became known, disparagingly, as 'von Lettow-Fallback'.

All three British divisions were on the Central Railway by the end of August. Dar-es-Salaam was doomed and the port of Bagamoyo had already been taken in a neat operation on 15 August. The garrison numbered 400, and had a *Königsberg* gun in its arsenal, but it fell to just 300 troops supported by the *Mersey* and *Severn*, and by a seaplane that dropped bombs on the German positions. Naval bombardment and rudimentary aerial bombing also preceded the fall of Dar-es-Salaam, which surrendered on 4 September.

It had taken the British just weeks to reopen the Northern Railway earlier in the year. The longer Central Railway had been more systematically destroyed by the retreating Germans – no fewer than 60 bridges had been blown up. Getting it up and running again would take into October, but the course of events suggested the lights were going out on von Lettow's resistance. Smuts saw an opportunity to end the war with one more effort.

The 6in. guns of the monitor HMS *Severn* had previously helped destroy the *Königsberg* on the Rufiji Delta. In August 1916 they played their part in the assault on Bagamoyo. (Chronicle/Alamy)

PART IV: THE GERMANS WITHDRAW

German forces now numbered around 9,000, with 1,500 Europeans and 7,500 *askari*. Half of this force had crossed over the Rufiji by the end of October. Tired of watching von Lettow withdraw, Smuts attempted to cut off one of his lines of retreat. The ports of Kilwa and Lindi had been taken, threatening to get behind von Lettow's force. Smuts now strengthened the garrison at Kilwa, and Hannyngton's Brigade occupied nearby Kibata. His presence goaded von Lettow into a response – on 6 December, the German commander sent Lieutenant Apel, formerly of the *Königsberg*, to attack the fortified government station there.

As well as at least nine companies, Apel had with him a *Königsberg* gun, two mountain guns and a howitzer. The station was surrounded by

The 1917 offensive

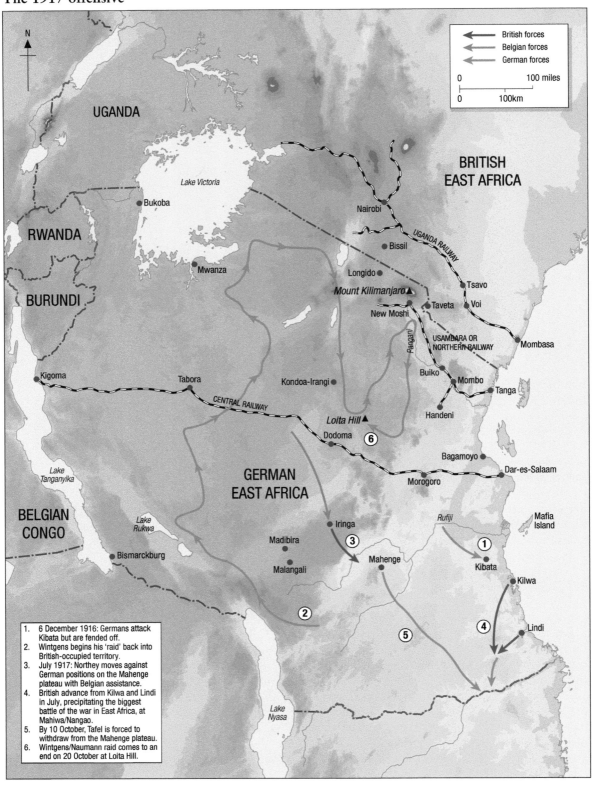

Legend:

←	British forces
←	Belgian forces
←	German forces

Scale: 0 — 100 miles / 0 — 100km

1. 6 December 1916: Germans attack Kibata but are fended off.
2. Wintgens begins his 'raid' back into British-occupied territory.
3. July 1917: Northey moves against German positions on the Mahenge plateau with Belgian assistance.
4. British advance from Kilwa and Lindi in July, precipitating the biggest battle of the war in East Africa, at Mahiwa/Nangao.
5. By 10 October, Tafel is forced to withdraw from the Mahenge plateau.
6. Wintgens/Naumann raid comes to an end on 20 October at Loita Hill.

the Matumbi Hills, and the occupying troops were caught off guard, not having expected the Germans to be able to bring up artillery. Apel's attack was committed and the battle continued to the end of the year before the Germans disengaged.

Among the defending troops were men of the newly arrived Gold Coast Regiment, West African soldiers called upon to plug the gaps left by the Indian, South African and British troops who had evaporated under the double assault of climate and disease. Back in the summer, the Gold Coast troopers, having fought in Togo (then known as Togoland) and Cameroon, were told they would be shipping out to the other side of the continent. The news was met with 'war dances and clamorous rejoicings'. By 5 July 1916, the regiment was ready to move. Four 'double companies' had been formed (A, B, G and I) along with a pioneer company, two 2.95in. guns and 12 machine guns. Under Lieutenant-Colonel R. A. de B. Rose, they numbered 1,428 men, including 36 British officers.

Hauled aboard the transport ship *Aeneas* six at a time, bundled in canvas sails (an experience the men apparently enjoyed hugely), they set sail as a partial eclipse of the sun took place, which could be viewed as either a good or a bad omen, depending on your outlook. After a brief stop at Durban (the British appeared to have learned their lesson following the miseries endured by Indian Expeditionary Force B), *Aeneas* docked at Kilindi, the port at Mombasa, on 26 July.

Following this light-hearted opening to their campaign, however, the spirit of the regiment was sorely tested after its arrival in East Africa. A sudden downpour drenched the men as soon as they had disembarked, and a train journey that took them up to an altitude of 9,000 feet chilled them to the bone. Many cases of pneumonia, some of them fatal, ensued.

On a nine-day march the men were then coated with the fine red dust of East Africa, until they looked like an army of terracotta soldiers, and at night they were tormented by the cold. Bush fires could spring up at any time, often catching ox teams and burning them to death. As the

The Gold Coast Regiment, experienced troops from West Africa, arrived to swell the depleted British ranks in July 1916. Here, a gun crew in their distinctive headgear poses for the camera. (*The Gold Coast Regiment in the East African Campaign*, 1920)

Nigerian troops on the march. The Nigerian Brigade, four regiments strong, joined their fellow West African troops from the Gold Coast by the end of 1916. (Public Domain)

oxen also began to fall victim to the tsetse fly, morale in the regiment plummeted: 'You could not get a grin out of them at any price,' one officer commented.

The regiment's first encounters with the Germans underlined the confused nature of bushfighting. On 12 September, G Company came under heavy fire and later worked out that the respective lines of the opposing forces had been just 50 yards apart. The Germans could stage an ambush at any moment and companies could find themselves lost in tall elephant grass – it sometimes took hours for the main body to be rediscovered. Improvized explosive devices were usually a 4in. shell, buried nose-down, with a plank set on a pivot and slanting up to just under the road surface. When stepped on, the plank would make contact with the nose of the buried shell.

As usual, however, it was the country itself that was the real enemy. Maps were rudimentary or non-existent, and rivers were often discovered by an officer 'by the simple process of pitching headlong into it'. Even accurate maps would have had dubious value, however. The vanguard of the regiment could wade through a river in neck-deep water, while the rearguard would be only knee-deep and the next day the river would have dried up completely. By 28 November, only 19 officers were still fit for duty and G Company had been disbanded, with its remnants used to bolster the remaining three double companies.

At the same time, Nigerian troops were also on their way as the war increasingly became an African affair. Rumours of deployment to the east had started back in May, but it was 15 November before the first troops sailed. The Nigerian Brigade numbered four regiments, totalling 3,400 men. New rifles were issued to the soldiers after they embarked, and they were drilled in their use en route to East Africa, where they started to reach Dar-es-Salaam on 10 December.

The Nigerians saw their first action on the Mgeta River on 1 January 1917, and very quickly earned a reputation. In contrast to the established pattern of the war so far, where troops would advance and retire freely, the Nigerians tended to take a position and stubbornly hold it. The Germans were in equal parts puzzled and intimidated, with one captured officer questioning the British about these new troops, 'who neither advanced nor retired, but just sat down and defied anyone to move them'.

East and West African soldiers got on well. As they passed each other, the Nigerians would call out 'Jambo!', meaning 'good morning', while the King's African Rifles would reply with 'Yumyum!', which meant 'cannibal', but was used affectionately (rumours that the Nigerians were cannibals were actually believed by the East African soldiers).

The Nigerians had a similarly trying introduction to East Africa as their Gold Coast comrades. On 25 January 1917, the wet season began, and by all reports it was an exceptionally heavy one. Based at Mkindu, the Nigerians' world quickly contracted into a nightmarish semi-existence, as rations were first halved and then, on 13 February, quartered. Several died after digging up roots to eat and inadvertently poisoning themselves. Maps, when the regiment came to finally move again, were of their standard quality. 'A nice map of Switzerland with a few African names upon it would have been just about as useful,' one British officer commented.

Mwanza, on Lake Victoria, pictured around 1907. The town was briefly the supposed target of the Wintgens/Naumann Raid in the latter half of 1917. (Haeckel collection/ullstein bild via Getty Images)

At least one man was about to escape from the misery of campaigning in East Africa. In early 1917, Smuts was given a plum position at the Imperial War Conference, in London. Acting as South Africa's representative at the conference was undoubtedly a great honour, but it also allowed him to save face while withdrawing from command. The war had not gone according to his plan, but he felt the need to declare that he had gained a victory, in order to avoid the impression that he had been bested by von Lettow. Smut's declaration that the war was effectively over would cause problems for the men who followed him, who had to deal with the reality of a war that was very much alive and kicking.

The first man to step into Smuts' boots was Hoskins, the commander of the 1st Division. With Smuts' declaration of victory still ringing in people's ears, Hoskins found himself in the extraordinary position of being asked to give up troops for service in other theatres, when he actually badly needed reinforcements. In March, he had a paper strength of 40,000 men, but only 12,000 of those were simultaneously considered 'reliable' and fit for service.

Hoskins was not long for the job, however. Such was the regard in which Smuts was held, any comments about officers left behind in East Africa would be listened to. Although no firm record exists, it appears that he made disparaging comments about Hoskins' plans for the upcoming campaign, and the British general was relieved of his command. There was regret in East Africa, as Hoskins had been whipping his army into shape and optimism was building. Van Deventer was brought in to take command. He immediately recognized the need for more troops and begged for some of the South African units recently sent home to be returned to him. He received 7 and 8 SAI and would also get 10 South African Horse later in the year. The

A machine-gun detachment from the ranks of the *Königsberg* on the move in the Kilwa district. (Sueddeutsche Zeitung Photo/Alamy)

unfortunate South Africans could not have been pleased at being returned to East Africa, and the country offered its traditional welcome – out of 966 men in 7 SAI when it arrived in June, only 158 were fit for combat by November.

By this time, a peculiar sideshow was playing out, starring the renegade German Captain Wintgens (known to the British, rather charmingly, as 'Winkins'). Always independently minded, Wintgens took this to extremes in early 1917. Expected to move south to link up with Kraut's detachment, Wintgens instead took off on an astonishing raid northwards, back into territory long ago conceded by the retreating Germans. Although it is not clear why (or exactly when) he made the decision, the 'Wintgens Raid' made a mockery of the idea that the campaign in East Africa was over.

By the end of May, Wintgens was too ill to continue on his flight of fancy, but having personally surrendered to Belgian forces near Tabora, the raid continued under the leadership of Captain Heinrich Naumann. Under Brigadier-General W. F. S. Edwards, 'Edforce' (comprising 3,000 Indian, Cape Corps, KAR and Nigerian troops, and supported by four battalions of Belgian *askari*) would give chase to Naumann's 500 men – a perfect realization of von Lettow's overall strategy.

Naumann threatened Mwanza, as far north as Lake Victoria, and he was not to surrender until 20 October, by which time he commanded just 173 officers and men, and he became the only German commander in East Africa to be tried after the war for crimes allegedly committed during the raid. Convicted, his death sentence was commuted and he returned to Germany in 1939.

Van Deventer planned to restart offensive operations in July 1917 and von Lettow consolidated his position to oppose British advances inland from Kilwa and Lindi. Although well aware that his eventual retreat was inevitable (supply dumps were prepared further south in anticipation and he was scouting Portuguese East Africa as well), his goal remained to frustrate the British forces ranged against him.

July brought three main thrusts from the British. Northey moved against the German positions on the Mahenge Plateau (now commanded by Tafel and numbering around 3,000), with support from Belgian troops. Brigadier-General P. S. Beves (standing in for Hannyngton, who was ill) led an advance from Kilwa and O'Grady struck out from Lindi, with the aim of cutting off von Lettow's escape route southwards.

Opposing the move of Beves was Captain von Liebermann, who chose to make a stand at Narungombe with eight companies, well entrenched on twin hills flanking the road. The British attacked on 19 July, numbering close to 2,000 men (double Liebermann's strength), and a day of brutal fighting followed. British casualties were heavy and bush fires were ignited by mortars, sometimes dooming wounded men to an agonizing death.

Despite his disadvantage in numbers, Liebermann's men performed so well that the British felt they were on the verge of defeat when the Germans unexpectedly withdrew – believing he was under attack from a much larger force, Liebermann had called an end to the battle. Von Lettow, on his way to reinforce Liebermann with four companies, could only curse his luck at failing once more to inflict a decisive defeat on his enemy, but the British were unable to resume their advance for two months. The Gold Coast Regiment had suffered particularly badly during the day-long battle, losing 158 killed and wounded out of a strength of less than 800.

To the west, Northey's men, aided by the fast-moving Belgian troops, continued to harry Tafel, who was forced to withdraw from the Mahenge Plateau on 10 October, with around 2,500 men left. Von Lettow waited anxiously for this detachment to re-join his main body of troops, but in the meantime, he was faced with another opportunity to inflict a serious defeat on the British pressing in from the east.

The initial British advance from Lindi had been roughly treated by the defending Germans, under Wahle, who had inflicted losses of over 250 on O'Grady's column. O'Grady was forced to halt his advance until a major offensive could be planned for October. By then, the two main British concentrations had undergone a change of leadership. Hannyngton, fit again, returned to lead the troops originating from Kilwa, while Beves moved to take command of the Lindi force from O'Grady. Where O'Grady was respected by the Germans, Beves was not – von Lettow saw him as the epitome of the unimaginative general who would continually hurl his men into wasteful frontal assaults. This change of command would directly shape von Lettow's decisions in what turned out to be the most costly battle of the entire war in East Africa.

The Battle of Mahiwa/Nyangao

Beves' 'Linforce', divided into two columns (No. 3 and No. 4 columns, each numbering 1,100 men), began to push Wahle's nine companies slowly backwards along the Lukuledi River. The Germans were following their usual practice of putting up enough resistance to exact a toll on the advancing British while not risking encirclement, but the picture changed dramatically when Hannyngton sent 1,500 men of the Nigerian Brigade, under Lieutenant-Colonel Mann, southwards.

Von Lettow had been inactive for a week when he received news of a British column on the move. This was the Nigerian Brigade, and he recognized the danger to Wahle's force as the intention was clearly to cut off his line of retreat. Von Lettow therefore embarked on a forced march with five companies (4, 10, 13 and 21 FK, along with 8 SchK) and two guns, to come to Wahle's assistance, picking up more troops on the way and concentrating at Mahiwa.

At this stage, there was a clear misunderstanding of the situation at British HQ. On the morning of 15 October, Beves was informed that the Germans were 'now much shaken, and a determined advance on your line… will probably have decisive effect'. Far from being shaken, the Germans were preparing to make a major and determined stand.

The Nigerian Brigade, comprising the 1st, 2nd and 4th regiments, was not moving as quickly as hoped. Stifling heat and confusion over which road to take towards Mahiwa had conspired to slow them down, and on 14 October they were given fresh orders to detach one of their regiments to Nyangao to outflank Wahle. Only two regiments were therefore to advance on Mahiwa, and Mann took the decision to leave his baggage, ammunition supplies and ambulances at Namupa Mission before pressing on.

The 1st Regiment set out on 15 October, accompanied by the Gambia Company and a section of the Nigerian Battery, but was forced to dig in a mile from Nyangao by fierce German resistance. Mann's column, meanwhile, advanced on Mahiwa on the 15th. With the 2nd and 4th regiments, a section of the Nigerian Battery, a section of Stokes mortars, 16 machine guns and 16 Lewis guns, they set off at 05:30hrs.

A Nigerian machine-gun position. Although the image claims to be from the action at Mahiwa, it is almost certainly a staged photograph. (Public Domain)

Mistakenly believing that Mahiwa had a limited German presence, Beves had continually pressed upon Mann the need to advance boldly. The Nigerians would be 'the cork in the bottle' to prevent Wahle from withdrawing in the face of Linforce's advance... but with the arrival of von Lettow's men, Mahiwa was held in strength.

By 11:00hrs, 15 Company had been forced to halt its progress at the vanguard of the Nigerians' advance. They dug in and awaited developments, until Beves once more ordered them to push forward. A frontal assault being impossible, a flanking move was attempted by 16 Company, which was quickly overwhelmed by a German force (Lieutenant Methner's 4 SchK), which may have been moving up for an attack of its own. Carriers fled, taking with them the company's reserve ammunition, and a withdrawal was soon essential as first the machine guns and then the Lewis guns fell silent. Von Lettow then threw the newly arrived companies of *Abteilung* von Ruckeschell (10 and 21 FK) into the attack. The men of 16 Company somehow managed to retire in good order, but they suffered 40 per cent casualties.

Shaken by the unexpected strength of the German attack, Mann pulled his men back to where he was already setting up a defensive perimeter with his main force, entrenching and preparing for action the following day. During the night, the Nigerian troops could hear Germans moving into position on the western and northern sides of their position, and the morning of 16 October found the Nigerians all but surrounded. Patrols ascertained that the Germans were in strength to the south, east and west, while patrols were blocking the escape route northwards. Mann was able to radio headquarters

THE NIGERIANS AT MAHIWA, 15–16 OCTOBER 1917

Shown here are the events of the Battle of Mahiwa.

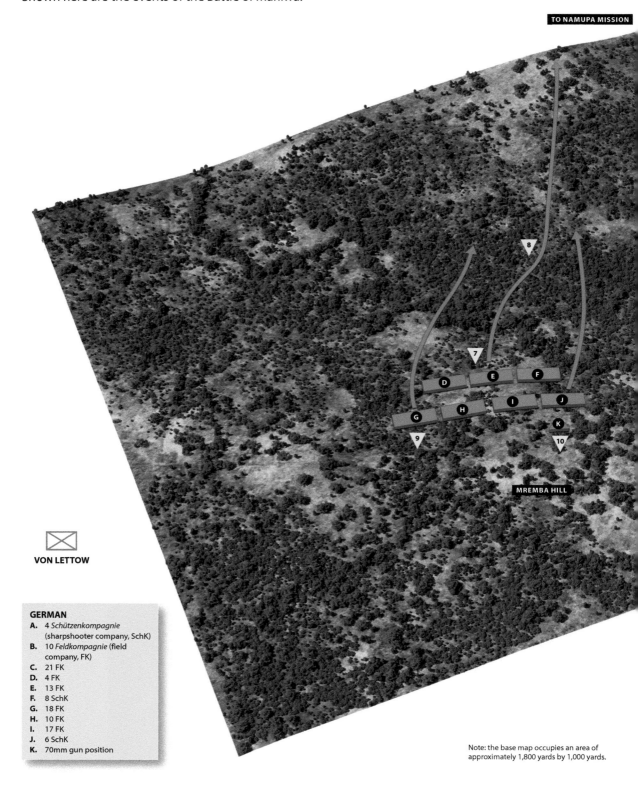

TO NAMUPA MISSION

MREMBA HILL

VON LETTOW

GERMAN

A. 4 *Schützenkompagnie* (sharpshooter company, SchK)
B. 10 *Feldkompagnie* (field company, FK)
C. 21 FK
D. 4 FK
E. 13 FK
F. 8 SchK
G. 18 FK
H. 10 FK
I. 17 FK
J. 6 SchK
K. 70mm gun position

Note: the base map occupies an area of approximately 1,800 yards by 1,000 yards.

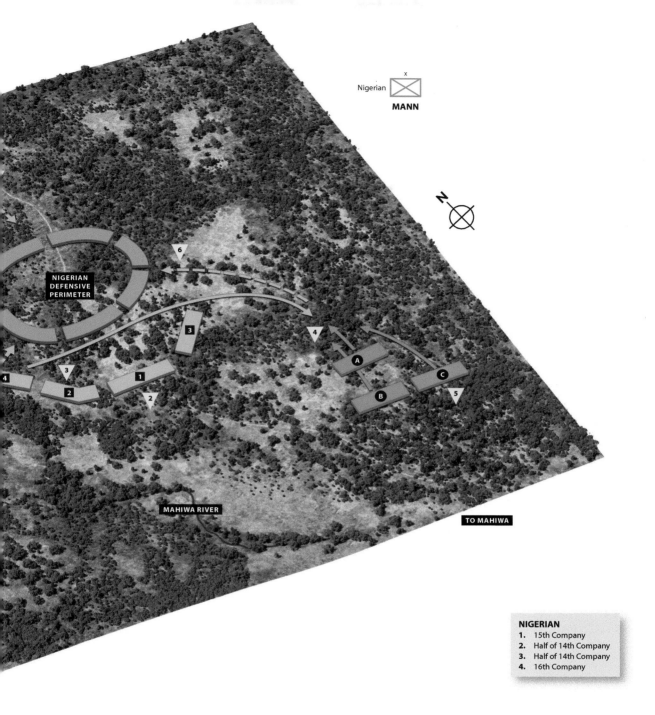

Nigerian

x

MANN

NIGERIAN
DEFENSIVE
PERIMETER

6

3

4

3

1

A

C

4

2

B

5

2

MAHIWA RIVER

TO MAHIWA

NIGERIAN
1. 15th Company
2. Half of 14th Company
3. Half of 14th Company
4. 16th Company

EVENTS

1. The 2nd and 4th Nigerian regiments advance towards Mahiwa.

2. The 15th Company, in the vanguard, is stopped by strong German resistance and reinforced with the 14th and 16th companies.

3. The 16th Company is sent on a flanking march, aiming to get around the Germans' easternmost flank.

4. This movement is countered by 4 SchK, which pins the 16th Company down.

5. The newly arrived 10 and 21 FK are thrown into the attack, and 16th Company withdraws after suffering heavy losses.

6. The advanced Nigerian companies are pulled back to a defensive perimeter being set up on a hill, and entrenchments are built.

7. Around noon on 16 October, *Abteilung* Göring crosses the Mahiwa River intending to attack the western side of the Nigerian position.

8. As von Lettow watches, this body of men instead veers off northwards, having spotted the approach of the 1st Nigerian Regiment.

9. Heavy reinforcements back up *Abteilung* Göring as the 1st Nigerians are stopped in their tracks.

10. The afternoon sees an artillery bombardment torment the Nigerians as they await rescue.

A Kashmir Mountain Battery at Mahiwa. Although Indian troops received mixed reviews for their performance in East Africa, the Mountain Batteries were highly respected and fought bravely at the Battle of Mahiwa/Nyangao. (Public Domain)

and request that the 1st Regiment be sent with the brigade's ammunition and supplies, left at Namupa Mission, and Beves gave permission. Shortly afterwards, the radio line was cut by the German patrols to the north, and the Nigerians were cut off.

That afternoon an artillery bombardment of their hastily dug entrenchments commenced. A 4.1in. *Königsberg* gun was inaccurate and its shells sailed harmlessly over the positions, but a closer 70mm gun proved far more effective. To make matters worse, no parados had been constructed behind the Nigerian breastworks, so shells falling inside the circular position proved lethal. By 16:00hrs, the 70mm gun started to strike the trenches held by 14 Company, with shots spaced just a minute apart, until a withdrawal became unavoidable. No sooner had the section of trenches been vacated than the artillery bombardment ceased and the Germans launched an attack, but the shaken men of 14 Company returned to their defensive works just in time to prevent the entire position from unravelling.

Meanwhile, the two columns of Linforce were attempting to break through the main body of Germans under Wahle, and the battle developed into a grim diptych, as Beves struggled to break through to relieve the Nigerians. Von Lettow, however, saw the battle differently. Beves' determination to rescue the Nigerians offered the German commander the opportunity he had been waiting for, and he gradually withdrew troops from positions pinning down the Nigerians to reinforce the main front against Linforce.

Von Lettow explained his decision in chilling terms: 'I... used all my available strength in such a way that the enemy by the increasing fierceness of his frontal attack was bleeding himself to death.' Von Lettow admitted that he was breaking from his usual tactics, but justified his decision in terms of what he knew of Beves' command style. Having watched him attacking at Reata back in March 1916, he knew that the general 'threw his men into action regardless of loss of life and did not hesitate to try for a success, not by skilful handling and small losses, but rather by repeated frontal attacks which, if the defence held its ground and had anything like adequate forces, led to severe losses for the attack'. Von Lettow's reasoning was sound, but Beves was actually too far away to control the shape of the battle. Nonetheless, the British attack did, for the most part, take the form of the expected frontal assaults.

The 1st Nigerian Regiment had gathered the requested supplies at Namupa Mission but were held up on their march to Mahiwa by a savage assault from *Abteilung* Göring (4 and 13 FK along with 8 SchK), which was steadily reinforced by 18, 10 and 17 FK and 6 SchK. The regiment was unable to break through to relieve its fellow Nigerians and, worse, the carriers abandoned their loads as they fled from the German attack. As the Nigerians were pushed back there was a danger that the brigade's ammunition reserve would fall into German hands, but the 1st Regiment managed to hold its ground and then recover most of the supplies.

By the morning of 17 October, Linforce was within a mile of Mahiwa, with concerted attacks slowly pushing the Germans back, but as relief for the Nigerians seemed within reach, von Lettow launched a well-timed counterattack that sent the British back to the day's starting positions. The Nigerians had actually been ordered to advance and push the Germans back, an order that betrayed a total misunderstanding of the brigade's tenuous position. With ammunition running out and the men suffering from acute hunger (only half a pound of rice had been eaten by each man in the past 24 hours) the situation was critical. The 3rd Regiment, called up from the reserve, was ordered to relieve the 1st Regiment and joined forces with them near Namupa Mission on the morning of 17 October, meaning the entire Nigerian Brigade was involved in the battle.

It was not until 18 October that O'Grady's column broke through, although even this success came with a dispiriting footnote. As the need to break through to the beleaguered Nigerians became desperate, the few remaining men of the 25th Battalion Royal Fusiliers were flung into the attack. Following two years of service, the 'Frontiersmen' had seen their numbers whittled away until only 126 were left to answer the call, and they were cut to pieces when they stumbled into a German machine-gun position. Only 50 survived what would be the regiment's last action of the war.

The stage was set for yet more savage fighting the next day, but on 19 October it was discovered that the Germans had broken off the engagement. Leaving the British in command of the battlefield made this, technically, a British victory, but it had come at a staggering cost. Out of around 4,500 men engaged, the British had suffered nearly 1,500 casualties. Von Lettow's losses, however, made it difficult for him to claim a victory either. Out of 1,500 men he had lost 500, and he had used up 850,000 rounds of ammunition. As had happened at Jasin nearly three years earlier, the German commander was forced to accept that he could not afford any more battles on this scale. The time had come for a dramatic change of strategy.

THE 25TH ROYAL FUSILIERS AT MAHIWA (PP. 82–83)

As the British attack on the morning of 18 October developed, Brigadier General O'Grady performed a personal reconnaissance and found the 126 men of the 25th Royal Fusiliers were temporarily without orders.

The British advance was over ground contested the day before, and fires caused by the intensity of the fighting had cleared the tall grass in front of the German positions (**1**).

O'Grady intended for the small band of fusiliers to come up in support of the 30th Punjabis (on the right of No. 4 Column), but whether they misunderstood their orders, or intentionally swung to the right to support 3/2nd KAR (on the left of No. 3 Column), the fusiliers found themselves moving parallel to the German line and made an easy target for German gunners.

At least two machine guns were reported as opening fire, supported by riflemen (**2**). Depicted is a German gun crew, with a German *vize-feldwebel* (or senior sergeant) manning the gun (**3**) and a German officer watching on (**4**). The officer wears no symbol of rank, as was common – many of the clothes worn by von Lettow's men by this stage of the war were hand-made and uniformity (including on the matter of headwear) was impossible.

A trail of dead and wounded was left in the wake of the fusiliers as they hurried to find cover, eventually taking shelter in clumps of dense bush (**5**). Out of sight of the British line, they could then only wait for rescue, unable to break cover.

Unfortunately for the few remaining fusiliers, it was German *askari* who found them first, and a bayonet charge destroyed the remainder of the regiment. Although a few managed to fight their way out and return to the British lines, the majority of those caught in the bush were killed.

PART V: THE FINAL STAGE

On 17 November, von Lettow decided that he could no longer maintain his army. Small though it was, the difficulty in finding supplies made it all but impossible to continue as he had been. He therefore took the difficult decision to cut his force down to the bone, retaining little more than a symbolic 'army' with which to maintain his defiance of the British.

Medical staff undertook a rigorous physical examination of the men under his command and ruled out anyone with any form of disability or sickness. In this way, no fewer than 7,700 men were deemed unfit for further service, including 700 Europeans. Stripped down to just 14 companies, with 37 machine guns, this much-reduced force marched over the Makonde Plateau en route to Portuguese East Africa. A further pruning was undertaken before the next stage of the campaign began, with more troops failing their medical, including Captain Loof of the *Königsberg*. On 25 November, von Lettow crossed the Rovuma with 278 Europeans, 1,700 *askari* and 3,000 porters (the number of porters is estimated, as no official records were kept). There would be a boost when Tafel crossed the Rovuma and joined forces with von Lettow, but it would still be a pathetically small force, and the question remained: what exactly could von Lettow hope to achieve with it?

As it happened, Tafel's force never linked up with von Lettow. Although he crossed the Rovuma (with over 1,300 men) just two days after von Lettow, he was unable to locate his commander and came to an independent decision. He crossed back into German East Africa and surrendered (a patrol under the renowned Captain Otto did manage to find the main German force).

Help from another, rather outlandish direction, had also failed to reach the beleaguered Germans by this point. An operation codenamed 'the China Show' had intended to resupply von Lettow via Zeppelin. It was a wild scheme, but it appears to have had a chance of succeeding. Although vast in size, a Zeppelin's payload was limited, but given the reduction in size of the German force it would have made a difference. A new breed of giant Zeppelin had been developed, and L59 was chosen for the mammoth voyage. It was packed with 300,000 rounds of rifle ammunition, 57,500 rounds of machine-gun ammunition and 30 new machine guns, along with a generous supply of spare parts and sacks of badly needed medical supplies.

It was to be a one-way trip, with the L59 slated for cannibalism after landing. Its skin could be torn up for bandages while its frame could be used to fabricate radio masts and other structures. There is debate over whether or not British intelligence managed to infiltrate this scheme and send confusing radio messages to the airship as it made its slow progress southwards, but when the Germans abandoned the Makonde Plateau, the game was up. That was the targeted landing site and by the time von Lettow crossed the Rovuma, L59 had already turned sadly back towards Germany.

Max Loof, former captain of the *Königsberg*, saw his war come to an end when he was deemed unfit to remain with von Lettow for the crossing of the Rovuma into Portuguese East Africa. (Public Domain)

Von Lettow-Vorbeck in Portuguese East Africa

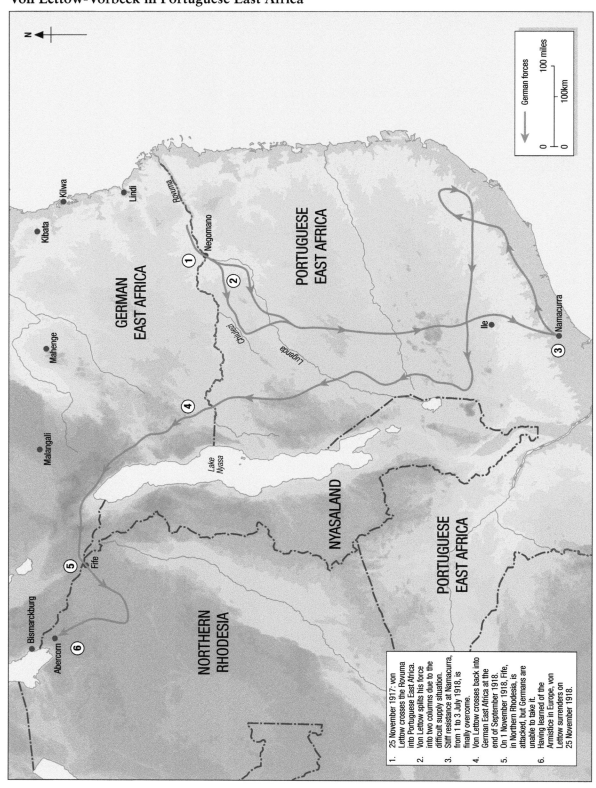

1. 25 November 1917: von Lettow crosses the Rovuma into Portuguese East Africa.
2. Von Lettow splits his force into two columns due to the difficult supply situation.
3. Stiff resistance at Namacurra, from 1 to 3 July 1918, is finally overcome.
4. Von Lettow crosses back into German East Africa at the end of September 1918.
5. On 1 November 1918, Fife, in Northern Rhodesia, is attacked, but Germans are unable to take it.
6. Having learned of the Armistice in Europe, von Lettow surrenders on 25 November 1918.

The Zeppelin L59 takes off on its mission to resupply the German Army in East Africa. Whether or not the journey was ever possible, the crew turned back for home while still well short of their goal. (Sueddeutsche Zeitung Photo/Alamy)

Von Lettow's first target after crossing into Portuguese territory was the post at Negomano. Well garrisoned, with 1,200 Portuguese soldiers, it took 24 hours of savage fighting for the Germans to crack it, but the rewards were substantial. As well as six machine guns, they found a quarter of a million rounds of ammunition. Von Lettow then split his force in two, with Wahle leading a column along the Chiulesi River and von Lettow a second column along the course of the Lujenda (both tributaries of the Rovuma).

The British response to this latest gambit by the German commander was predictable. With the German Army now in Portuguese territory, the British might have been tempted to hand over responsibility for finishing it off. But the Portuguese had proved to be almost worse than useless, and the idea of letting von Lettow run freely south of the Rovuma was anathema to British commanders who by now were more than a little obsessed with their elusive quarry.

Much is made of the overwhelming superiority of numbers enjoyed by the British, and it is true that they greatly outnumbered their opponent, but with so many garrisons to maintain, not to mention often ludicrously long supply lines, the picture was not so clear-cut. Van Deventer had around 7,500 men actually available to chase von Lettow, and they were always slower, as they refused to live off the land, as the fast-moving German *askari* did. Despite the limited resources available, a sense of desperation had crept into British planning by this stage. Inflicting losses on the dwindling German force was considered the prime objective. The cost entailed became of secondary importance, but it was a cost that was rising. By the end of the year, the Nigerian Brigade was withdrawn, as well as most of the remaining Indian troops (two Mountain Batteries remained).

Perhaps unsurprisingly, as the war entered yet another new year, both sides were nearing the end of their resources. Von Lettow's men had suffered a slump in morale as soon as they left their own territory, and they fought a number of small-scale encounters that served to erode their numbers still

Nigerian troops crossing the Rovuma in pursuit of the Germans. The Nigerians' time in East Africa was drawing to a close – they would be withdrawn from the front line by the end of 1917 – but they had served with great distinction and won the admiration of friend and foe alike. (Public Domain)

further. By the end of March, van Deventer expected von Lettow to lead his men back into German East Africa. Instead, he took them even further south. British forces followed but were unable to catch him as he rampaged from post to post in search of supplies. The Gold Coast Regiment was the next to be withdrawn, worn out after less than two years of campaigning. The regiment had suffered 215 deaths from enemy action and another 270 from disease, with 725 wounded, 567 already invalided home and 13 missing. It had been a brutal experience for the men who had reacted with joyful war dances when informed they would be travelling eastwards. The large number of medals bestowed upon the regiment may have been some consolation.

Portuguese forces were proving completely incapable of standing their ground. At Ile, the defending troops simply ran as soon as the Germans were spotted, surrendering a huge amount of supplies – more, in fact, than von Lettow's small force could carry off. Great quantities were burned to prevent them from being of use to either the Portuguese or British.

At Namacurra, however, stiffer resistance was offered. With the assistance of two King's African Rifles companies, commanded by Colonel Gore-Browne, three Portuguese battalions stood and fought against three German companies under Captain Müller. The assault started late on 1 July and was still raging on the afternoon of 3 July, by which time von Lettow had brought up his main force. The Portuguese units had been steadily pushed back and resistance finally crumbled, with the remnants of the defenders being forced to escape over the Namacurra River. At least a hundred men drowned, including the unfortunate Gore-Browne. Spoils including champagne fell into German hands and were put to good use. An air of unreality had descended on the campaign as it entered a stage known by the Germans as 'the Opera War'.

By the second week of August, van Deventer was ready to renew his pursuit. The weather was bad, as the short rains had started, but putting an end to the campaign appeared to be in sight. Nevertheless, one of the columns pursuing von Lettow had chased him for 1,600 miles before it had to admit defeat, by the end of September. At the same time, German forces were evaporating. In a series of confused, chaotic engagements in the first weeks of September, von Lettow lost more than 200 men. More than 200 of his soldiers also fell victim to a strange virus (which von Lettow referred to as a 'lung epidemic'), and he had no alternative but to leave sick and badly wounded by the wayside as he was driven on by his pursuers. Most of these men were gathered up by the British, but many were simply never seen again.

The situation was untenable and at the end of September, von Lettow crossed back into German East Africa. The situation he encountered took him by surprise – he had almost total freedom. The pursuit had ground to a halt, worn down over the months of unending suffering. It had simply proved impossible to overhaul the faster German *askari* and the conclusion was unavoidable – von Lettow had won a strange kind of victory.

Cut off from the outside world, he knew little of what was happening in Europe, although it was understood that the war was going badly. In contrast to the limited horizons of trench warfare, von Lettow found he was free to go just about anywhere he pleased, and Tabora was the first place to catch his attention. He quickly discarded this idea for a far more ambitious one. Rather than re-tread the ground of former battlefields, he would take the war to new territories. He would invade Northern Rhodesia.

Perhaps a little intoxicated by the endless vistas opening up before him, there was even talk of marching all the way across the continent to the Atlantic. How realistic that was is debateable, but in any case, events were catching up with von Lettow far more effectively than the British had managed. On 1

An estimated 3,000 native carriers accompanied von Lettow on the last stage of his campaign. Many would join the *Schutztruppe* when casualties and disease thinned their ranks. (Amoret Tanner Collection/Alamy)

A rare moment of rest for the fast-marching *askari* is captured by von Lettow's adjutant. Routinely able to outpace their pursuers, the African troops remained undefeated until the end of the war. (Public Domain)

November he attacked Fife, in Northern Rhodesia, but this was not the same army that had terrorized German East Africa and set the Portuguese to flight at the mere sight of them. He had lost all his heavy artillery and was unable to overcome the stubborn defence mounted by the Northern Rhodesia Regiment. In the moment of his triumph, von Lettow was forced to realize that he had exhausted himself and his men every bit as much as the pursuing British. Carriers began to desert in large numbers. The German commander was strangely indulgent of this, perhaps recognizing that he had asked all he could of them. 'It would after all have been asking too much of human nature,' he wrote in his memoirs, 'to expect that these men, who had not seen their people for years, should now march straight through their native district.'

On 12 November, a British dispatch rider was captured, who informed von Lettow that the war in Europe was over. It took a while for the news to sink in, and von Lettow admitted to hoping the war had ended favourably for Germany, but further resistance in East Africa was now meaningless. The following day, von Lettow learned that he had been ordered to surrender unconditionally, and he immediately realized what this meant: 'This... showed the desperate situation of the Fatherland. Nothing else could account for the surrender of a force still maintaining itself proudly and victoriously in the field.'

With no further reason to run, pursuing British forces (the 1st Battalion 4th King's African Rifles) finally caught up with him. The young officer commanding, Colonel Hawkins, admitted candidly that he would have been unable to pursue von Lettow further, and asked if the Germans had any supplies they could share with his hungry troops.

On 25 November, von Lettow surrendered his battered little army to Brigadier-General W. F. S. Edwards at Abercorn. He had 155 Germans with him, having at one time counted 3,000 among his numbers. Equally symbolic of the course the war had taken was the fact that there was not one modern German rifle among those surrendered, and only six German machine guns. Von Lettow's single remaining piece of artillery, along with the 30 other heavy and light machine guns and 1,071 modern rifles with his army, were either Portuguese or British in origin. His *askari* numbers were down to 1,156, while only 1,598 carriers remained.

Paul von Lettow-Vorbeck left German East Africa on 17 January 1919. It was five years to the day since he had arrived at Dar-es-Salaam.

AFTERMATH

The immediate aftermath of the war was simple. Britain took control of the bulk of German East Africa, which was known as British Tanganyika before becoming Tanzania after gaining independence. Belgium took control of Burundi and Rwanda, while the Portuguese were given the Kionga Triangle. Germany's dreams of an African empire stretching across the entire middle of the continent lay in ruins.

Far more important than this, however, was the human cost. Von Lettow had been able to frame his war aims in terms of diverting British men and materiel from the European theatre, and this had been achieved to a certain extent, but at a truly terrible cost. A total of 126,972 British

Von Lettow's men were able to stay out of reach of the slower British forces largely because of their willingness to live off the land, which had a devastating impact on the territory they marched through. (ullstein bild via Getty Images)

Von Lettow became something of a folk hero for a German population desperate for good news as the war ground to its conclusion. This poster, encouraging people to buy war bonds, uses a heroic image of the 'African Kaiser', complete with his signature. (Library of Congress)

troops had served during the conflict, drawn from all over the vast empire. Of these, 11,189 had died. Of von Lettow's redoubtable *askari*, an estimated 2,000 died from wounds or sickness. Belgian casualties were around 5,000 in total with just over half of those dying, while Portugal lost over 5,500 men, mostly from disease.

These numbers, which seem low but represent significant percentages of the men involved, are dwarfed by two other figures. The number of native carriers that perished is uncertain, but is estimated at more than 90,000. When it is borne in mind that for the most part these were paid either very little or not at all, the losses among the million or so men who served in this manner are nothing short of scandalous.

Britain's policy of supplying its columns via tortuously long supply chains made their armies slow-moving – too slow to catch up with von Lettow's *askari* – but it spared the local populations from at least some of the miseries of war. Von Lettow's policy of living off the land, and often laying waste to supplies he could not make use of to deny them to the British, spared nobody. An estimated 300,000 civilians died in German East Africa during the war, often as the result of famine sparked by the passage of military forces.

As soon as he had surrendered, having evaded the British for four years, von Lettow was caught by another enemy. The Spanish flu, which may have been the mysterious virus that had stricken his men in Portuguese East Africa, hit with a vengeance. Just weeks later, 300 of his surrendered men had died, a mere drop in the ocean of two million estimated deaths in sub-Saharan Africa from one of the worst global pandemics in history. Many local histories record this with a simple but chilling phrase: 'There came a darkness.'

THE BATTLEFIELDS TODAY

Most of the battlefields of German East Africa have been largely undisturbed since the fighting more than a century ago. Tours of many are available, including Salaita Hill, which offers the chance to explore the German trenches and imagine the view as the soldiers of the 2nd South African and 1st East African Infantry brigades advanced.

Tanga has grown, but you can still view the beach where the hapless British troops landed prior to their disastrous assault on the town, as well as the curve of the railway cutting, so stubbornly defended by the Germans. The Urithi Tanga Museum also offers an excellent experience for anyone interested in the colonial history of the town.

The waterways of the Rufiji Delta, a hellish place of confinement for the crews of the *Königsberg* and the ships sent to destroy her, can be enjoyed in comfort from any number of riverboat cruises, while a living piece of the war can still be found on the waters of Lake Tanganyika, where the *Goetzen*, refloated and renamed, now operates as a passenger ferry under the name MV *Liemba*.

The MV *Liemba*, previously known as the *Goetzen* and once master of Lake Tanganyika, now follows a more peaceful existence as a passenger ferry on the same waters it once ruled. (Daniel Hayduk/AFP via Getty Images)

FURTHER READING

The standard text on the East African Campaign is *Tip & Run: The Untold Tragedy of the Great War in Africa*, by Edward Paice. Paice's depth of research is second to none, and he deals in tremendous detail with the movements of the armies and the battlefield manoeuvres. If any criticism can be made, it is that sometimes the level of detail is almost overwhelming and the reader can find it difficult to get a clear picture of the overall situation.

More entertainingly written, but sadly lacking in the academic rigour that Paice brings to his work, is *African Kaiser: General Paul von Lettow-Vorbeck and the Great War in Africa*, by Robert Gaudi. Gaudi has written a rollicking page-turner, but wherever details (on troop numbers or casualties, for instance) differ from those provided by Paice, it is invariably Paice who proves to have been correct. The sheer readability of Gaudi's tale, however, makes it useful for the casual reader.

Various texts from those with first-hand experience in the campaign are available, none more important than *My Reminiscences of East Africa*, by von Lettow-Vorbeck himself. His reminiscences don't always match up with others, but that is only to be expected in personal accounts. Unit histories, including those of the Nigerian Regiment (*With the Nigerians in German East Africa*, by W. D. Downes) and the Gold Coast Regiment (*The Gold Coast Regiment in the East Africa Campaign*, by Sir Hugh Clifford), offer fascinating insight into the day-to-day experiences of the men who fought. For those wishing to delve down to an even more granular level, many unit diaries are available for research at The National Archives in Kew, or via digital download.

Also available at The National Archives is the unpublished second volume of the official history of the war. Complete with draft chapters, maps and dispatches, this is a veritable treasure trove.

Osprey has previously visited the campaign in two excellent titles. *Armies in East Africa 1914–18*, by Peter Abbott and illustrated by Raffaele Ruggeri, gives detail on the composition of the armies involved in the war, while *King's African Rifles Soldier versus Schutztruppe Soldier*, by Gregg Adams and illustrated by Johnny Shumate, takes a closer look at some of the fighting men from both sides.

INDEX

Figures in **bold** refer to illustrations.

Adler, Captain 37
Aeneas, HMS 71
Africa **4 (map)**, 6
Aitken, Major-General A. E. 26, 27, 29, 31, 34, 35
Alexandre Delcommune 23–24, 50
Apel, Lieutenant 69, 71
armoured cars 52, **54–56**
Auracher, Dr 29

Bagamoyo, fall of 68, **69**
Baron Dhanis 51
Baumstark, Captain 28, 34
Belgian Congo 16, 19
Belgian forces 9, 21, 50, 50–51, 64–65, 75, 92
Belgium 16, 91
Beves, General P. S. 75, 76, 80
Boer War 26
bridges 40, **40**
British East Africa 5, 23
British forces 15–16, 26 39, **60**, 91–92
    armament 15
    commanders 10–11, **10**
    Gold Coast Regiment 21, 71–72, **71**, 75, 88
    King's African Rifles **14**, 15, 16, 21, **21**, 25, 37, 45, **67**, 88
    Loyal North Lancs 31, 45, 51–52, 59, 60
    machine guns **77**, **82–84**
    Nigerian Brigade 72, 72–73, 76–77, **77**, 80–81, 87, **88**
    orders of battle 16–18
    plan 20–21
    reinforcements 42, 51–52
    Royal Fusiliers 45, 49, **49**, 81, **82–84**
    scouts **61**
    sickness 41–42, 51–52, 60–61
    strength 20, 87
    supply chains 92
Bukoba, raid on, campaign 45, 49–50, **49**
Burundi 50, **64**, 91

campaign
    action at Kibata 69, 71
    action at Lake Tanganyika 64–65
    advance through the Nguru Mountains 68
    Anglo-Belgian relations 64–65
    assault on Saisi 50

assault on Salaita Hill 52–53, **53 (map)**, **54–56**, 57, 59
attack on Taveta 23
attack on the *Königsberg* **43**, 44–45, **44**
Battle of Jasin 35–37
Battle of Kondoa-Irangi 61–64
Battle of Mahenge Plateau 75
Battle of Mahiwa/Nyangao 18, 76, 76–77, **77**, **78–79 (map)**, 80–81, **80**, **82–84**
Battle of Negomano 87
Battle of Tanga 16–17, 26–31, **26**, **27**, **28**, **30**, **32–33 (map)**, 34–35, **34**, 93
Belgian advance 64
British offensive 23–37
cost 91–92
fall of Dar-es-Salaam 68
final stage 85, **86 (map)**, 87–90, **89**
German raids 39–41
German reorganization 39
German resupply 41, **41**
German withdrawal 69, **70 (map)**, 71–84
hunt for the *Königsberg* 42–44
invasion of German East Africa 60
invasion of Northern Rhodesia 89–90
Norforce 67–68, **68**
Northern Railway offensive 66
opening moves 23–26
Portuguese contributions 65–66
raid on Bukoba 45, 49–50, **49**
the railway war 38–57, **39**, **40**
second assault on Salaita Hill 59–60
South African offensive 57, **58 (map)**, 59–69, **70 (map)**
Tanganyika Expedition 50–51, **51**
Wintgens/Naumann Raid 73, 75
Caulfeild, Captain 28, 29
Central Railway 67, 68–69, 69
Chatham, HMS 25, **25**
Christiansen, Lieutenant 41
chronology 8–9
City of Winchester 7

Dar-es-Salaam 7, 23, 68
Dartmouth, HMS 25
disease 15, 16, 41, 60–61, 65–66, 89, 92

Driscoll, Lieutenant-Colonel Daniel Patrick 49

Edwards, Brigadier-General W. F. S. 90

Falkenstein, Count 39
Fox, HMS 28, 29, 30

German Central Africa 19, **19**
German East Africa 5, 6–7, 19, 20, **20**, **22 (map)**, 60, 89, 91, 93
German forces 13–15, **13**, **42**, **91**
    askari 13–14, **14**, 15, 20, 36, 37, 39, **65**, 69, 90, **90**, 92
    commanders 11
    machine guns 37, 57, 74, **82–84**
    morale 87–88
    orders of battle 16–18
    organization 14
    reorganization 38–39
    resupply 41, **41**, 62
    sickness 89
    strength 13, 14, 69, 90
    surrender 13, 90
German South-West Africa 36
Gil, General Ferreira 65–66
Goetzen, SS 50–51, **51**, 64–65, **64**, 93, **93**
Goliath, HMS 29

Hannyngton, Brigadier-General J. A. 66
Henry, Commandant Josué 50
Herero Uprising **6**, 11
Hermann von Wissmann 23
Hoskins, Major-General Arthur Reginald 10–11, **10**, 60, 66, 74
Hyacinth, HMS 43

Indian Expeditionary Forces 15–16, 16, 20–21, 23, 28 37, 41–42, 51–52, **52**
    assault on Salaita Hill 53, 57
    Battle of Tanga 26–31, 34–35, **34**

Jasin, Battle of 35–37

Kepler, Major 37
Kibata, action at 69, 71
Kilimanjaro, Mount 39, **60**
Kitchener, Lord 37
Koehl, Captain 59
Kondoa-Irangi, Battle of 61–64
Konduchi 23
Königsberg, SS 7, 15, **24**, 36, 93

attack on **43**, 44–45, **44**, 46–48
guns 45, **45**, 51, **51**, 62, **62**, 66, 68, 69, 80
hunt for 24–25, 42–44
Kraut, Major Georg 39, 59, **59**, 66, 68
Kronborg, SS 43

Loof, Captain Max 36, **85**

machine guns 15, **37**, 52, **54–56**, **57**, 74, 77, **82–84**
Mafia Island 36, 43
Mahenge Plateau, Battle of 75
Mahiwa/Nyangao, Battle of 18, 76, 76–77, **77**, **78–79 (map)**, 80–81, **80**, **82–84**
Malleson, Brigadier-General Wilfrid 52, 59, 61
Mann, Lieutenant-Colonel 76–77, 80
Marie (blockade-runner) 62
Meinertzhagen, Captain Richard 27
Merensky, Lieutenant 29–30
Mersey, HMS 43, 44, 45, **46–48**, 68
Mimi 51
Mombasa 25, 28
motorized transport **63**
Mwanza 50, 73, 75

native carriers **89**, 90, 92
Naumann, Captain Heinrich 75
Negomano, Battle of 87
Northern Railway 21, 26, 61, **62**, 66, 69
Northern Rhodesia 50, 89–90
Northey, Brigadier-General E. 67–68, **68**, 76

O'Grady, Brigadier-General 60, 75, 76, 81, **82–84**
orders of battle 16–18

Pegasus, HMS 7, 45, 52, 62
Peters, Carl 5, **5**
Portugal 16, 91
Portuguese East Africa 7, 19, 24, 65, 85, **86 (map)**, 87–89
Portuguese forces 21, 65–66, 87, 88, 92
Pretorius, Piet 44
Prince, Tom 11, **30**, 31, 34
prisoners of war **34**

quinine 39

Royal Navy 6, 7, 39
Rubens (blockade runner) 41, **41**

Rufiji Delta 24, 36, 42, 93
Rwanda 50, 64, 91

Saisi, assault on 50
Salaita Hill, assault on 52–53, **53 (map)**, **54–56**, 57, 59
second assault on 59–60
Schnee, Heinrich 6–7, **7**, 19, 23, 65
Severn, HMS 44, 45, **46–48**, 68, **69**
Sheppard, Brigadier-General S. H. 66
Short Seaplane 64–65, **64**
Smith-Dorrien, Horace 51–52
Smuts, Jan Christian 12, **12**, 52, 74
advance through the Nguru Mountains 68
flanking march 61
and German withdrawal 69
launches offensive 59
Northern Railway offensive 66
plan 21, 57
second assault on Salaita Hill 59–60
tactics 57
South African forces 16, 21, 41–42, 51–53, 66
2nd South African Infantry Brigade **54–56**, 57
5th South African Infantry Regiment **54–56**, 60
7th South African Infantry Regiment 60, 75
armoured cars 52, **54–56**
commanders 12, **12**
East African Infantry Brigade 53
machine guns 52
Norforce **67–68**, **68**
strength 16, 57, 59
South-West Africa **6**
Spanish flu 92
Spicer-Simson, Lieutenant-Commander Geoffrey Basil 51, 64
Stewart, Brigadier-General James 23, 35, 45, 49, 59, 61

Tanga, Battle of 7 16–17, 20–21, 26–31, **26**, **27**, **28**, 30, **32–33 (map)**, 34–35, **34**, 50, 93
Tanganyika, Lake 7, 24, 50, 50–51, **51**, 64–65, **64**, 93, **93**
Taveta 23, 25–26
Tighe, Michael 'Mickey' 10, **10**, 42, 45, 61
assaults on Salaita Hill 52–53, **53 (map)**, **54–56**, 57, 59, 60
Battle of Jasin 35–37
Togo **21**

Toutou 51
Uganda Railway 7, **38**, 39, **39**, 40
Usoga, HMS **49**

van Deventer, Jacob 'Jaap' 12, **12**, 59–60, 61–62, **62**–64, 66, 67, 68, 74–75, **75**, 88, **88–89**
Victoria, Lake 45
von Hammerstein, Captain 37
von Langenn-Steinkeller, Major Erich von 25, 64
von Lettow-Vorbeck, Lieutenant-Colonel Paul 7, 11, **11**, 15, **59**, **92**
aims **19**
assault on Saisi 50
assault on Salaita Hill 52
attack on Taveta 23
Battle of Jasin 36, **36**–37
Battle of Kondoa-Irangi 62, 62–64
Battle of Mahiwa/Nyangao 76, 77, 80–81, 81
Battle of Tanga 27–28, 30–31, 34, 35
invasion of Northern Rhodesia 89–90
Iron Cross award 62
and the loss of the *Königsberg* 45
move against Mombasa 25
and Norforce 68
and Northern Railway offensive 66
plan 19–20
in Portuguese East Africa 85, **86 (map)**, 87–89
preparations 23, 25–26
reorganizes forces 38–39
second assault on Salaita Hill 59–60
strategy 7
surrender 13, 90
tactics 19–20, 39–40, 81
task 24
withdrawal 69
von Liebermann, Captain 75

Wahle, Kurt 11, **11**, 39
Wapshare, Brigadier-General Richard 35, 42
water supplies 40–41
Weymouth. HMS 25
Wintgens, Captain Max 64
Wintgens/Naumann Raid 73, 75

Zeppelin *L59*, resupply mission 85, 87